OSPREY MILITARY CAMPAIGN SERIES 23

KHARTOUM 1885

GENERAL EDITOR DAVID G. CHANDLER

OSPREY
MILITARY

CAMPAIGN SERIES 23

KHARTOUM 1885

GENERAL GORDON'S LAST STAND

DON FEATHERSTONE

◀ *General Gordon,*
'the heroic defender of
Khartoum', as apotheo-
sized in the pages of the
Illustrated London
News *of 14 February*
1885.

First published in 1993 by Osprey
Publishing Ltd,
59 Grosvenor Street, London W1X
9DA.

ISBN 1-85532-301-X

Produced by DAG Publications Ltd
for Osprey Publishing Ltd.
Colour bird's eye view illustrations by
Cilla Eurich.
Cartography by Micromap.
Mono camerawork by M&E
Reproductions, North Fambridge,
Essex.
Printed and bound in Hong Kong.

Many of the pictures in this volume
are from contemporary editions of
The Illustrated London News.

▲ *This R. Caton Woodville drawing is dated 31 January 1885, so it could depict any minor action of the 19th Hussars who were with the Desert Column during that month which saw the Battles of Abu Klea and Abu Kru.*

CONTENTS

Egypt and the Sudan: Operations 1883-1885°

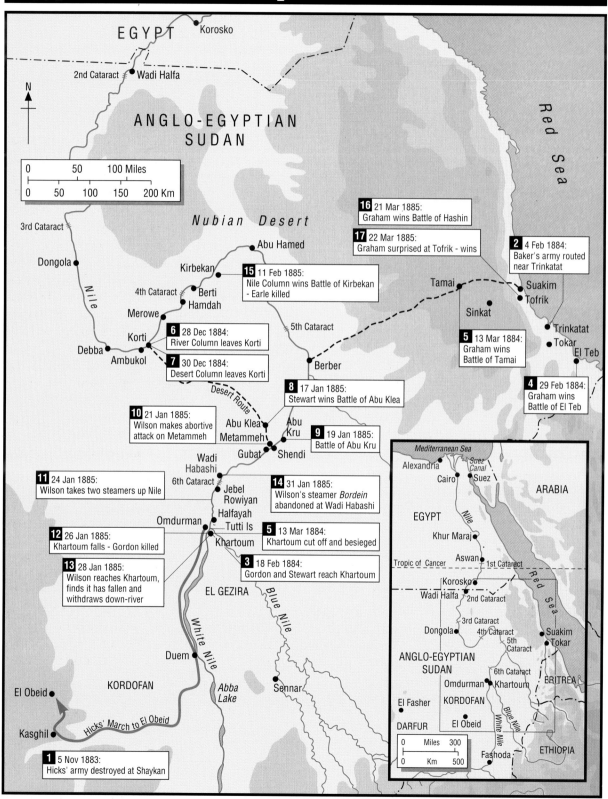

EGYPT
Korosko

2nd Cataract ● Wadi Halfa

N

ANGLO-EGYPTIAN
SUDAN

| 0 | 50 | 100 Miles |
| 0 | 50 | 100 | 150 | 200 Km |

Nubian Desert

16 21 Mar 1885:
Graham wins Battle of Hashin

17 22 Mar 1885:
Graham surprised at Tofrik - wins

2 4 Feb 1884:
Baker's army routed
near Trinkatat

3rd Cataract

Dongola ●

Abu Hamed ●

Kirbekan ●

15 11 Feb 1885:
Nile Column wins Battle of Kirbekan
- Earle killed

Tamai ●

Suakim
Tofrik

4th Cataract ● Berti
● Hamdah

Merowe ●

5th Cataract

Sinkat ●

Trinkatat
Tokar
El Teb

Korti ●

6 28 Dec 1884:
River Column leaves Korti

5 13 Mar 1884:
Graham wins
Battle of Tamai

Debba ●
Ambukol ●

7 30 Dec 1884:
Desert Column leaves Korti

Desert Route

Berber ●

4 29 Feb 1884:
Graham wins
Battle of El Teb

8 17 Jan 1885:
Stewart wins Battle of Abu Klea

10 21 Jan 1885:
Wilson makes abortive
attack on Metammeh

Abu Klea
Metammeh

Abu
Kru

9 19 Jan 1885:
Battle of Abu Kru

Gubat
Shendi

Mediterranean Sea

Alexandria ●
Suez
Canal
Cairo ● ● Suez

ARABIA

Wadi
Habashi
6th Cataract

14 31 Jan 1885:
Wilson's steamer *Bordein*
abandoned at Wadi Habashi

EGYPT

11 24 Jan 1885:
Wilson takes two steamers up Nile

Jebel
Rowiyan
Halfayah

Khur Maraj ●

Omdurman ●
Tutti Is

12 26 Jan 1885:
Khartoum falls - Gordon killed

Khartoum

5 13 Mar 1884:
Khartoum cut off and besieged

Aswan ● ● 1st Cataract

Tropic of Cancer

13 28 Jan 1885:
Wilson reaches Khartoum,
finds it has fallen and
withdraws down-river

3 18 Feb 1884:
Gordon and Stewart reach Khartoum

Koroska ●

Wadi Halfa ● 2nd Cataract

EL GEZIRA

Blue Nile

3rd Cataract

Dongola ● 4th Cataract
5th
Cataract

Suakim
Tokar

White Nile

Duem ●

KORDOFAN

*Abba
Lake*

Sennar ●

ANGLO-EGYPTIAN
SUDAN

6th Cataract

Omdurman ● Khartoum

ERITREA

El Fasher ●

KORDOFAN

El Obeid ●

Blue Nile

El Obeid ●

DARFUR

El Obeid ●

Kasghil ●
Hicks' March to El Obeid

| 0 | Miles | 300 |
| 0 | Km | 500 |

Fashoda ●

ETHIOPIA

1 5 Nov 1883:
Hicks' army destroyed at Shaykan

THE RISE OF THE MAHDI IN THE SUDAN

The two campaigns fought by the British in the Sudan, in 1884-5 and 1896-8, were far more than an attempt to relieve Khartoum and the eventual reconquest of the country. For almost two decades Great Britain had been involved, directly and indirectly, in the military affairs of the Sudan, whose history during the late 19th century can be divided into four distinct periods:

1881-8 — The rise and defeat of Mahdism
1881-3 — The defeat of the Egyptian Army
1884-5 — The first British involvement
1896-8 — The reconquest of the Sudan.

The Sudan

The Arabic name for the Sudan is Baled-el-Sudan — 'Land of the Blacks', and the events under consideration occurred in the eastern (Anglo-Egyptian) part of the country, stretching about 1,400 miles from the southern frontiers of Egypt to Uganda and the Congo (now Zaire), and from the Red Sea to Wadia. The capital is now Khartoum, although after its capture by the Mahdi in 1885, the distinction of being the principal city was transferred to Omdurman. The northern part of the area is very arid, consisting mostly of scrub desert, rocky outcroppings and wadis, with large areas of sava grass; trees are mostly thorny acacia, and mimosa grows in close profusion. The southern part is scrub jungle and swampland. The most important feature of the Sudan is the mighty and dangerous River Nile, with six almost impassable cataracts between Egypt and Khartoum. Generally very hot, the climate is perverse and temperatures can drop to freezing during the night.

The Peoples of the Sudan

In the north the Hamitic Arabs, in the south the Negroes; the former being divided into several major peoples — Beja in the area around Suakim; Ababdeha in the north; Bisharin south of Wadi Halfa; north of Debba the Kababish, the Hassaniyeh and the Shaguyeh near Khartoum. South of that city was the homeland of the Baggara people, and the Amara were the major tribe near Abu Hamed.

All of these were subdivided into numerous tribes — the Hadendowa were part of the Beja, and the Taaisha were a division of the Baggara: there were the Beja-Hadendowa, Baggara-Taaisha, the Jaalin, the Danaqla, the Batashin, Berberin, Barabra, Allanga, Duguaim, Kenana, Awadiyeh, the Hamr-Kordofan, Darfureh, Monassir, Sowarab, the Hauhau-hin, Robatab, Base and Shukreeyeh. It could truly be said that the Mahdi's recruiting ground was the entire male population of the Sudan.

History of the Sudan in the late 19th Century

This vast and inhospitable land, grudgingly watered by the Nile, had lain festering throughout the century, under the unchallenged, unkindly, unprofitable and unwise rule of her neighbour Egypt. In eight major garrisons and many lesser posts, 40,000 soldiers of the Egyptian Army held the country in corrupt and unhappy submission, stoking up fires of hatred that would inevitably burst into blazing rebellion. Early in 1881 the general unrest began to crystallize around the name of an obscure man of religion, Mohammed Ibn Ahmed el-Sayyid Abdullah, in his retreat on the island of Abba in the Nile, about 150 miles upstream from Khartoum.

Proclaiming himself the long-expected Mahdi, the Guided One of the Prophet, he preached that the Sudan was to be purged of its Egyptian oppressors, and her people brought back to the purity of the true faith. Soon, the Egyptian government, installed by the British after the Arabi Pasha revolt of 1882, found itself hard-pressed to

▲ *The Mahdi (Mohammed Ibn Ahmed el-Sayyid Abdullah), 1844-85. This warrior-priest of humble origin emerged in 1881, rapidly to become the undisputed leader of the entire Sudan, revered by all as a reincarnation of the Prophet. Before he died on 22 June 1885 (probably of typhus or smallpox) he had defeated every British and Egyptian challenge and had reigned supreme in the Sudan.*

maintain authority in the Sudan, being forced into a series of abortive operations against the Mahdi's swelling hordes of followers until finding itself with only token garrisons to defend isolated posts at Sennar, Tokar, Donagla and Berber.

The Mahdi's first battle victory was in August 1881 at Abba, where his 311 ill-armed Arabs cut a much larger Egyptian force to pieces; in October Rashid Bey marched to Khur Maraj with 1,200 men, to be annihilated by a force swollen to 8,000 warriors; on 29 May 1882 another Egyptian army, lured into the interior to Jebel Jarrada, were destroyed in their zareba at night by a Mahdist army now 15,000 strong.

The next objective was El Obeid, rich capital of

Kordofan, defended by 6,000 Egyptian troops whose commander, Mohammed Sayyid, on 1 September 1882 hanged the Mahdi's emissaries who had offered surrender terms. Now numbering 5,000 cavalry and 50,680 foot, the Mahdists assaulted the town but were thrown back with heavy losses by the disciplined fire of Egyptian Regulars' Remington rifles. Abandoning former edicts that his troops should use only 'traditional' weapons such as spears and swords, the Mahdi, now allowing the use of the rifles captured from previously defeated Egyptians, tightened the siege and El Obeid fell on 17 January 1883; high-ranking officers were executed and all the surviving troops were pressed into the Mahdi's service.

Every reverse encouraged the rebellion which now turned into civil war, with followers flocking to the Mahdi's banner; from Kordofan Province where his influence was greatest, the Mahdi extended his domains until he controlled most of western Sudan. At the same time his principal lieutenant, Osman Digna, was active among the tribes along the Red Sea coast, and by the autumn of 1883 several Egyptian garrisons were cut off and under siege.

The fall of Kordofan, the richest province in the Sudan, convinced the Egyptian government that an expedition would have to be sent to suppress the rebellion and, the British being unwilling to co-operate, sought a man to lead it. In late January 1883 Abd el Kader, the new Governor-General of the Sudan, appointed a retired Indian Army officer, Colonel William Hicks, to the post of Chief of Staff.

The Destruction of Hicks Pasha

Colonel William Hicks had begun service in 1849 in the Bombay Army, fought in the Mutiny of 1857, and saw service in Abyssinia with Napier in 1868. Courageous and energetic, but with little command experience, 52-year-old Hicks began organizing the troops available to him for his Sudan expedition. In April 1883 he led out a force of four and a half battalions of infantry, some mounted Sudanese Bashi Bazouk mercenaries and four Nordenfelt machine-guns. On 29 April, at Jebel Ain, he was confronted by a sizeable Mahdist force with numerous cavalry. In square, with rocket tubes, howitzers and the Nordenfelts pouring out a deadly fire at close range, they repelled the attack at a cost of only seven casualties; the enemy leaving more than 500 dead on the ground, including twelve Amirs and their leading chief, Amr-el-Makachef.

Elated, the Egyptian government now began planning the reconquest of Kordofan, believed by Hicks to be premature, but his doubts were overcome by the government which persisted in its hasty and flawed policy. The Egyptian Army in the Sudan had always been made up of the rejects and cast-offs from the army in Cairo, a posting to the Sudan being accepted as a form of punishment for some military misdemeanour. Seeking to improve the quality of his troops, Hicks asked for troops from the British reorganized and retrained Egyptian Army; refusing his request, Cairo sent him 3,000 inferior men, several hundred of them being rejects from the new Egyptian Army, and 1,800 of Arabi Pasha's former mutineers. After threatening to resign, Hicks decided to do the best he could with what he had, and by late August the expedition was consolidated by the arrival of 4,000 camels and a cavalry force of men untrained to ride.

On 9 September the Hicks Pasha Expedition marched out of Omdurman towards Duem, 110 miles distant, the objective being the recapture of El Obeid in the heart of rebel-held Kordofan. The force comprised:

- 7,000 Regular cavalry
- 500 Untrained cavalry
- 400 Mounted Bashi Bazouks
- 100 Chain-mailed mounted Cuirassiers
- 4 Krupp field guns
- 10 mountain guns
- 6 Nordenfelts
- 5,500 camels
- 500 horses

For more than two months the expedition contended with heat, thirst and constant Mahdist harassment, wracked by internal dissension among its senior officers. With first-rate intelligence and holding all the cards, the Mahdi sent Abd al Qadir with 1,000 horsemen to occupy the pools of al Birka, thus forcing Hicks to advance through the dense forests of Shaykan.

Meanwhile, the Mahdi utilized the time by

▲ *Colonel William Hicks (Hicks Pasha) had served in the Bombay Army from 1849, fought in the Indian Mutiny in 1857, and was on the Abyssinia Expedition with Napier in 1868. At the age of 52, engaged by the Egyptian Army as Commander-in-* *Chief of the Sudan Field Force, he took a scratch force of ill-trained Egyptian soldiers into the desert where, having been lured into the Shaykan forest, they were massacred on 5 November 1883.*

training his army for what he determined would be a decisive battle at a place of his own choosing. After the fall of El Obeid the Mahdi's army in Kordofan probably numbered 40-50,000 men including 3-4,000 horsemen and 5-7,000 trained riflemen (almost all Sudanese who had served in the Egyptian Army); the remainder were sword and spearmen. Five small brass mountain guns and almost 14,000 Remington single-shot breech-loading rifles had been captured in earlier engagements, and these were employed against Hicks.

Constantly harassed and under fire, his column stumbled through the almost impenetrable kittic thorn trees and tebeldis of the Shaykan forest. By 3 November the force was isolated in wild country without a secure line of retreat and, even if the final encounter had been less disastrous, it is doubtful if many would have got back to the Nile. On 5 November, deployed in a single large square which was broken as its front face was penetrated, the force was annihilated; Hicks and all his staff being killed.

Worse than a failure, the Expedition's defeat not only brought the Mahdi Krupp guns, Nordenfelts and thousands of Remington rifles, but vested the Mahdi with a degree of authority he had hitherto lacked, bringing thousands to his banner.

The Victorious Mahdi

By now the Mahdist rebellion was very powerful and had become a *jihad*, a dreaded Islamic holy war, with the alliance of hill tribes and Beja pastoral peoples strengthened by fierce Donagla horsemen and camel-mounted Baggara warriors from the desert lands. The Mahdi's Amirs ranged far and wide throughout the Sudan, browbeating apprehensive tribesman in their recruiting-drive for his ever-increasing army. The mail-clad Amirs from far-off Darfur — a primitive southern area — were rapidly bringing over their warriors to join the host, now that Slatin Pasha, the Governor of Darfur, had been forced to surrender.

Following the fall of El Obeid, Osman Digna, an influential and powerful Sudanese leader, declared the allegiance of himself and his Hadendowa followers to the Mahdiyya, as the Mahdist state was known. These Hadendowa tribesmen of the Beja were the 'Fuzzy-Wuzzies' of Kipling's poems.

The eastern Sudan, the area between the Nile and the Red Sea, now became hostile to Egypt, and the major caravan route between Suakim (on the Red Sea) and Berber (on the Nile) was no longer safe. The Egyptian garrisons of Tokar and Sinkat were besieged by Osman Digna at about the same time as Hicks' expedition was being destroyed; small Egyptian relief columns were destroyed on 26 October, 5 November and 2 December 1883.

▼ *Baker Pasha's force disembarking at Trinkatat on 30 January 1884, prior to setting out on their abortive attempt to relieve Tokar. They were destroyed near El Teb on 4 February.*

Gordon goes to Khartoum

The annihilation of Hicks' column, causing varying degrees of concern in Cairo, Khartoum and London, set in train a series of events leading to the decision to send General Gordon to Khartoum. On 4 January 1884, anticipating that the Egyptian government might request British aid to hold the Sudan, the British government proposed that the Sudan be abandoned; this brought about the resignation of the Egyptian government which was replaced by a ministry favouring the evacuation of Egyptian garrisons from the region. In London it was suggested that General Charles Gordon be sent to supervise such an evacuation because he was familiar with the region and its people, having administered it in the days of the Khedive Ismail. At this point the British press got wind of the affair, and as a result public opinion became clamorous in favour of sending Gordon to Khartoum. On two occasions, the last being on 10 January 1884, the proposal was rejected by Sir Evelyn Baring, the British Agent in Cairo, who felt strongly that Gordon was not the right man for the job, if only because Baring thought it undesirable that a Christian should be appointed to handle what was primarily an Islamic revolt.

On 15 January Gordon met Lord Wolseley and agreed to go to Suakim to assess the military situation in the Sudan; pressed by the government in London, Baring reluctantly agreed; seemingly General Gordon matched his request for a '...qualified British officer to go to Khartoum ... to conduct the retreat'. Beset on all sides by foreign advisers, the Egyptian government immediately accepted Gordon, and assumed that the British would now be responsible for any unforeseen consequences; in London the very opposite was assumed. The two governments charged Gordon with conflicting roles. His brief from London was that of an adviser who would report on the best methods of evacuation; the Egyptians appointed him Governor-General, an executive post concerned with the practical aspects of evacuation. Gordon himself seemingly planned, on arrival at Khartoum, to evacuate all Egyptian troops and any civilians who wished to leave the Sudan; the petty chieftains deposed at the time of the Egyptian takeover of the Sudan were to be restored, and would take possession of all arms and ammunition left by the vacating troops. It was not explained how this was to be done, what support he would require, or indeed if it were even possible in the face of the growing power of the Mahdi.

When considering Gordon's qualifications for the task, his colourful and well-known background must be taken into account, together with his almost unique experience of the region, having been Governor-General of the Sudan from 1877 to 1880, with headquarters in Khartoum. During that period he had been a most vigorous opponent of the slave-trade, and was liked by the people, who showed considerable respect for his authority and wisdom. Now in his early fifties, much of his life had been spent as a soldier in foreign parts; he was regarded as an authority on colonial warfare, and was known as 'Chinese' Gordon, a nickname acquired during distinguished service at the time of the Taiping Rebellion in China in 1863-4; he had also seen service in Russia during the Crimean War of 1854-5. A 'man of his era', Gordon was deeply religious and undoubtedly based his thoughts and actions on his Bible-readings. His unorthodox character and methods, and his charitable work for destitute youths endeared him to the church-going British public. His great devotion to whatever task he undertook impressed those working with him, who recognized him as being highly resourceful, if impetuous and inclined to occasional faulty judgement.

This, then, was the man who left London on 18 January 1884, a few hours after meeting the cabinet. With Lieutenant-Colonel J.D.H. Stewart of the 11th Hussars, he arrived in Cairo on the 25th, left there on the 28th and reached Khartoum on 18 February.

Baker Pasha fails to relieve Tokar

Recognizing the dire situation around Suakim, the Egyptian Army wished to use the 'new' army in the area, but being refused by the British they cobbled together a force of black volunteers and gendarmes, to be commanded by Major-General Valentine Baker. A hard-riding British cavalry officer who had fought in South Africa and the Crimea, Baker had been cashiered and sent to prison for indecently

assaulting a young woman on a train; subsequently fighting for Turkey in the war against Russia, he came to Cairo in 1882 to take command of the newly formed gendarmerie. This force assembled at Suakim in late December 1883, and on 26/27 January 1884 were transported by sea to Trinkatat from where they were to set out to relieve Tokar. The force consisted of some 1,200 Gendarmerie, 300 Massowa blacks, 800 of the newly raised black troops, 300 Bashi Bazouk Turks, 400 Egyptian cavalry, four guns and two Gatlings. This was an unimposing army, particularly as the gendarmes, who had mostly joined the police to avoid military service, were seething with resentment at being sent out of Egypt in a purely military role.

On 4 February Baker and his staff, riding in front, were unaware that his troops were not advancing in the organized square formation that had been ordered, but in a confused mass, highly vulnerable to the large numbers of swiftly moving Arabs who burst upon them. In a scene of utter chaos, the Egyptians abjectly lying down and offering no defence, the force was annihilated. Cutting their way through the swarming enemy, Baker and his staff joined what was left of the Turkish cavalry; a 5-mile fighting retreat took them to the beach, the Arabs holding back in fear of the guns of the ships lying off-shore. Leaving 96 officers and 2,250 men dead, Baker and the survivors returned to Suakim.

Realizing that relief was unlikely, Muhammad Tawfiq, commanding the besieged town of Sinkat,

◀ *R. Caton Woodville's graphic portrayal, within weeks of the events, of the destruction of the Hicks and Baker Pasha Expeditions in November 1883 and February 1884 respectively.*

on the coast, to mount a limited campaign.

Suakim was precariously protected by the guns of HMSS *Ranger* (gun-vessel), *Coquette* (gunboat) and *Euryalus* (corvette). From this Red Sea Division of the Mediterranean Fleet on 6 February, a force of 150 sailors and Marines and two Gatling guns was landed; a further 120 Marines were taken off the homeward-bound transport *Orontes*, and 280 more came up from Egypt in HMSS *Carysfort* (corvette) and *Hecla* (torpedo-depot ship).

Orders for a campaign to relieve Tokar were issued on 12 February and, on the following day, troops began to embark for Suakim. They came from garrisons in Egypt, Aden and India, and were to be commanded by Major-General Sir Gerald Graham, VC, KCB, sent from Egypt with Colonel H. Stewart commanding the cavalry and Sir Redvers Buller the infantry brigade. Learning of the fall of Tokar on his arrival at Suakim, Graham realized that his mission had changed from one of relief to one of offence, and that he was in a position to satisfy public demand for a victory. At Trinkatat from 26 to 28 February 1884 he concentrated the force listed below.

attempted a fighting withdrawal, spiking the guns and marching out in a huge square, women and children in the centre. Within a mile Osman Digna's forces were upon them and they were massacred on 8 February. Tokar surrendered fifteen days later.

Britain Enters the Fray

In Britain the political overtones of the defeats of Hicks and Baker aroused considerable passion as it became apparent that only the intervention of British troops could restore order in the Sudan and prevent the ultimate collapse of Egyptian rule in the East. Queen Victoria was in favour of sending an expedition, and – reluctantly – a signal was sent to Admiral Hewitt, who was commanding at Suakim,

Graham's force, February 1884	
1 Infantry Brigade (Buller)	*Men*
1st Battalion 75th Regiment	
(Gordon Highlanders)	730–750
3rd Battalion 60th Regiment	
(King's Royal Rifle Corps)	630
2nd Battalion 89th Regiment	
(Royal Irish Fusiliers)	350–400
26th Company Royal Engineers	100–150
6/1 Scottish Division Royal Artillery	
(eight naval 7pdrs mounted on Egyptian	
camel–battery carriages)	
2 Infantry Brigade (Davis)	
1st Battalion 42nd Regiment	
(Royal Highlanders – The Black Watch)	730–760
1st Battalion 65th Regiment	
(Yorks and Lancs)	450–500
Royal Marine Light Infantry	478
Naval Brigade (three Gatlings, three Gardner guns)	163
M/1 Royal Artillery (two 6cwt and two 8cwt guns	
borrowed from Royal Navy, on field carriages	
with limbers)	
Cavalry Brigade (Stewart)	
10th Hussars	250–300
19th Hussars	360–430
Mounted Infantry	120–150

13

OPPOSING COMMANDERS

The British Leaders

The Gordon Relief Expedition's commander, General Lord Wolseley (Sir Garnet), was the archetypal British Imperial General of the Victorian era and a noted 'trouble-shooter' who led expeditionary forces to all corners of the empire. Born in 1833, he had served in Burma, the Crimea, the Indian Mutiny, and was present at the storming of the Taku Forts in China in 1860. Created KCMG and CB in 1867, he had commanded the Red River Expedition in Canada in 1870; promoted to major-general, he had led the successful punitive expedition to Kumasi in Ashanti in 1873; Adjutant-General in 1882, he took command of a force in Egypt in that year, to defeat the Egyptian army of Arabi Pasha at Tel-el-Kebir on 13 September 1882. This led to British domination of the Egyptian

▲ General Sir Garnet (Lord) Wolseley, a notable 'trouble-shooter' of the Victorian era. He had led expeditions in all parts of the Empire — Canada, Ashanti and Egypt where he defeated Arabi Pasha in 1882. He was appointed commander of the Gordon Relief Expedition in 1884.

▲ General Sir Gerald Graham, VC, took part in the Crimean War, the storming of the Taku Forts in China, and commanded a brigade during the Egyptian War of 1882. He was the first British commander to encounter the Ansar, in the area of Suakim in 1883, and later was commander during the concluding operations of the Gordon Relief Expedition.

government and when, in the following year, the Sudan erupted in revolt culminating in Gordon's being trapped in Khartoum, Wolseley was the logical commander of a force to get him out.

Lieutenant-General Sir Gerald Graham, who commanded the British force that would be the first to encounter the Ansar in the Suakim area, was a distinguished soldier, having won the Victoria Cross while leading the ladder-party in an attack on the Redan at Sevastopol in the Crimea on 18 June 1855. He had been conspicuous at the capture of the Taku Forts in the China War of 1860; his well-known characteristic of always being in the thick of the fight (he was wounded on several occasions) had brought him rapid promotion so that he was a major-general in 1881 at the age of 50, and was chosen by his personal friend Lord Wolseley to command a brigade in the field during the Egyptian War of 1882. He was criticized for his tactics at Tamai, where he displayed errors of judgement in approaching too near the edge of a ravine, and in ordering The Black Watch to charge; due allowance should be made for the fact that he was in the thick of the fight and could see little. At the time, his errors were forgiven in view of his sound tactics in other battles.

Major-General Sir Herbert Stewart, KCB, born in 1843 and commissioned in the 37th Regiment (Hampshires) in 1863, subsequently joined 3rd Dragoon Guards in 1873; he served in the Zulu War of 1879 and the Transvaal War of 1881. Appointed Staff Officer to Sir Drury Lowe, commanding the Cavalry Division in the Egyptian War of 1882, he was prominent at Tel-el-Kebir; when General Graham went to Suakim, Stewart went with him and displayed soldierly qualities at Tamai, where his cavalry helped retrieve the fortunes of the day when the first square broke under the Arab charge; for this he received a KCB. He embarked upon the difficult duty of commanding the Desert Column with spirit and energy, leading to a victory that proved fatal to himself.

Colonel Sir Charles Wilson, KCB, KCMG took over command of the Desert Column when General Stewart was mortally wounded, the death of Colonel Fred Burnaby, at Abu Klea, making him the obvious choice. He took a steamer with troops up the Nile to Khartoum in an attempt to save Gordon, but was

▲ *Major-General Sir Herbert Stewart, KCB, commander of the Desert Force in the Gordon Relief Expedition. He had served with distinction in the Zulu War of 1879 and the Transvaal War of 1881,* *and had been prominent at Tel-el-Kebir during the Egyptian War of 1882. He was mortally wounded at Abu Kru, but remained with his troops, being carried in a litter. He died of his wounds about a month later.*

too late, for which he received considerable criticism. However, being an officer of the Intelligence Service sent by Wolseley to communicate with Gordon in Khartoum, he had never held command in the field, and was not fitted either by experience or by temperament to grapple with a critical situation.

Major-General William Earle, CB, CSI was the senior major-general in Egypt and commanded the River Column. Born in 1833, he had served with 49th Regiment at the Alma and Inkerman in the Crimea in 1854. His later career was with the Grenadier Guards and, at the commencement of the

▲ *Sir Charles Wilson, an officer of the Intelligence Service, originally sent by Wolseley to communicate with Gordon in Khartoum. On the death of General Stewart he took command of the Desert Column and, after an abortive attempt to capture Metammeh, took* *his troops up the Nile to Khartoum in river steamers in an endeavour to get Gordon out. On discovering that Khartoum had fallen he turned back, his steamers were wrecked and his men had to be rescued by Captain Lord Charles Beresford in* Safieh.

▲ *Major-General William Earle, CB, CSI, the senior general in Egypt. He commanded the Nile (River) Column, and was to be killed at* *the Battle of Kirbekan on 10 February 1885.*

Sudan operations, he was in command of the garrison at Alexandria; he attained the rank of major-general in October 1880. Said to be '...an officer of great and varied experience', he was to be killed at the Battle of Kirbekan on 10 February 1885.

Major-General Redvers Buller, VC, together with Lord Wolseley, had distinguished himself in most of the Empire's trouble-spots — China 1860, Red River Expedition 1870, the Ashanti War 1873, Kaffir War 1878 and the Zulu War of 1879 where he won the Victoria Cross for deeds at Hlobane

Mountain. An ideal brigade or perhaps divisional commander, he was to find himself out of his depth as commander-in-chief in South Africa against the wily Boers in 1899. He commanded 1 Brigade in Graham's force and was his second in command; his fellow-commander of 2 Brigade at El Teb and Tamai was General Davis.

Major-General Sir John McNeill, VC, CMG, whose zareba at Tofrik in the closing stages of the campaign was the scene of almost legendary colonial war-type fighting, had served in India and New Zealand; he was in command of 2 Brigade at Suakim, under General Graham.

Lesser actors in the drama included Lieutenant-Colonel J.D.H. Stewart, 11th Hussars, who accompanied Gordon to Khartoum and was

▲ *General Sir Redvers Buller, 1839–1908. His life was a series of military campaigns: he commanded the 1st Infantry Brigade in* *General Graham's force that left Suakim in February 1884.*

▲ *Captain Lord Charles Beresford, RN. A dashing officer who had disting- uished himself while commanding* **Condor** *at the bombardment of* *Alexandria, he was in command of the Naval Brigade in the Sudan.*

subsequently murdered by Arabs when the steamer en route from Khartoum to connect with the Nile Column, went aground. Captain Lord Charles Beresford, RN commanded the Naval Brigade in the Sudan Expedition. He was a dashing officer who had distinguished himself when commanding the gunboat *Condor* at the bombardment of Alexandria, and commanded the British force acting as police when that town was occupied. Lieutenant-Colonel Fred Burnaby, who was to be killed at Abu Klea, was a well-known and much-loved personality on the Victorian scene; a gigantic man, who had immortalized himself in a ride to Khiva, he intervened in every possible war of his day, taking an active part in the Russo-Turkish War of 1877 among others. At the time of the Sudan Campaign he was

commanding officer of The Blues, and took sick-leave in order to join the fighting in Egypt.

The Leaders of the Ansar

Besides his ability to arouse such fervour in his followers that, to a man, they were ready to die for him, the Mahdi also possessed more than a little military knowledge and skill, said to be derived from his study of Islamic military history, of the early days of Islam attended by much military glory; in effect, as would any student of early Islam, as the Mahdi studied so inevitably he learned the military tactics applicable to the type of warfare in which he was engaged. His ideas of organization were derived from the teachings of the religious schools and sects,

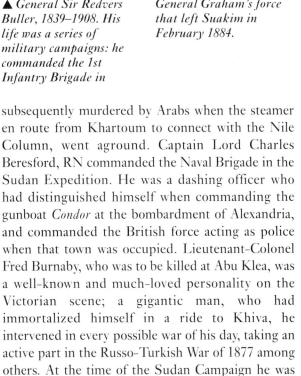

and from them he acquired the patience to wait for the propitious moment to deliver the fatal blow, at the same time exploiting to the full the confusion of the enemy; on many occasions one can discern a faultless instinct that marked his vital decisions. His autocratic rule was both crude and violent, punishments and atrocities being committed in the Name of God, and not patriotism. After the fall of El Obeid the Mahdi published a proclamation of the pattern of life to be undeviatingly followed by all who came under his banner; and it was ferociously enforced, with flogging to death, or amputation of limbs for the most trivial offences. Swearing and the taking of alcoholic drink were punishable by death; there was but one way to die honourably, and that was in battle in the holy service of the Mahdi.

The Mahdi's Lieutenants

Prior to the revolt a simple trader, al Zubayr wad Rahmah, organized an army of about 15,000 men and trained them with an extraordinary innate military skill; in its ranks were several future Mahdiyya leaders — al Zaki Yamal, Hamdan Abu Anja and al Nur Anqara. After conquering Darfur, al Zubayr was detained in Egypt where he had gone to meet the Khedive; the Mahdi's fury at the killing of Gordon stemmed from his desire to seek an exchange of Gordon for al Zubayr.

Perhaps the most effective leader in the field was Osman Digna, a former slave-dealer who had a substantial following among the tribes in the Suakim region and remained prominent in the Mahdiyya hierarchy under the Khalifa until Omdurman in 1898; he became senior Amir after the death of Abd al Rahman Mujumi. In eastern Sudan in 1884, Osman Digna led an army of more than 20,000 of whom 1,200 were armed with the Remington rifle; the army included the Bishareen Arabs who displayed a fanaticism that made them formidable opponents.

The Khalifa Abdallahi recruited Baggara Arabs and other tribes from the west around his black flag; the Khalifa al-Sharif's red flag drew warriors from the riverine peoples north of Khartoum, including Ja'aliyin and the Mahdi's own Danaqla; the green flag of the Khalifa Ali wad Hilu drew followers from the Dighaym, Kianan and al-Lahiwiyin Arabs of the

Gezira region between the Blue and White Niles.

Abd al Rahman wad al Mujumi led the force that annihilated Hicks and, leading the bulk of the assault troops, was in command at the siege of Khartoum. With him was Abu Qarja who led the bulk of the mounted forces; these two, with Muhammad wad Nubawi and Muhammad al Karim, were the council who, with the Mahdi, decided on the hour to attack and take Khartoum.

The Jihadiya were led by Hamdan Abu Anja; and Yunus al Dikhaim was another prominent Mahdist general. The Arab leaders at the battle of Abu Klea were Muhammad al Khair and Musa wad Hilu, who was killed; at Kirbekan, all three Arab leaders — Moussa wad Abuhegel, Ali wad Hussein and Hamid wad Lekalik — lost their lives.

▼ *Osman Digna. A Turkish/Sudanese slave-dealer, he commanded the Mahdists in the Red Sea region from the beginning of the revolt. Remaining prominent among Ansar leaders and becoming senior Amir on the death of Abd al Rahman Mujumi, was at the Battle of Omdurman in 1898.*

OPPOSING FORCES

The British Force, 1884-5

The British troops sent to the Sudan during this period were small expeditionary forces, organized in brigades and tasked with limited objectives; they were wholly inadequate to take on the full strength of the Mahdiyya, which was forced upon them in the long term. There were four separate theatres: the two eastern Sudan campaigns, fought around Suakim, presented no undue supply problems; but the Desert Column and the River Column planned to traverse the entire distance from the Egyptian border to Khartoum — which stretched the Army's resources to the very limits.

Organization of Units

British infantry regiments were organized into battalions each of which had eight 120-man companies; each cavalry regiment had four 160-man squadrons; an artillery battery generally had six guns with 113 men, horse batteries having 137 men. It was rare for companies, battalions or regiments to be fielded at full strength.

▼ *Most of the men had probably never seen a camel until reaching Egypt, and had to be trained from scratch.*

Here men of 19th Hussars test their steadiness by charging past a square of resting camels.

◀ *Drawn by Count Gleichen, who was serving with the Guards Camel Regiment in Stewart's Desert Column, these sketches capture the activities of the camel-mounted troops at various stages of the advance:*

Top: The departure from Korti, 30 December 1884.

Centre: A scouting party in advance of the main body, between Wadi Halfa and Dongola.

Bottom: A skirmish between the scouting force and a group of Arabs.

▶ *Top right: The Battle of Abu Klea, 17 January 1885: the attack on the left rear corner of the square where the Gardner gun jammed*

Mounted Infantry

There was a specially raised company of Mounted Infantry, formed of men from the Royal Sussex Regiment, The Black Watch, the Gordon Highlanders and the King's Royal Rifle Corps. Each contributed a detachment consisting of an officer, a sergeant, a corporal, a bugler and 27 men; the total strength of the Mounted Infantry being 130 men. At first they were mounted on Waler horses (an Australian breed supplied to the cavalry in India) and they trained on them, but at the last moment they had to hand them over to the Egyptian Army, receiving in return inferior ponies with old and rotten leather harness. The Mounted Infantry went by rail to Trinkatat and the ponies, all stallions, caused trouble by fighting and biting each other when in the trucks; they were even more unruly when travelling by ship, tied to the ship's rails.

The Camel Regiments

A camel-force was raised, with volunteers from fourteen regiments in both England and Egypt; in all, some twenty regiments were represented by the 500 officers and men who formed the Mounted Infantry Camel Regiment.

The Guards, the Heavy and the Light Camel Regiments

These were distinct and separate from other camel units, being drawn half from cavalry and half from infantry. In the Guards Camel Regiment there were detachments from the 1st, 2nd and 3rd Battalions Coldstream Guards; 1st and 2nd Battalions Scots Guards and the Royal Marines. The Heavy Camel Regiment was formed of selected men from 1st and 2nd Life Guards; The Blues; The Bays; 4th and 5th Dragoon Guards; the Royals; the Scots Greys; 5th and 16th Lancers — each unit providing two officers, two sergeants, two corporals, one bugler or trumpeter and 38 men. The Light Camel Regiment was drawn from the 3rd, 4th, 7th, 10th, 11th, 15th, 18th, 20th and 21st Hussars. Their strengths were: Guards, 17 officers, 302 men; Heavies, ten detachments formed of 23 officers, 438 men; Lights, nine detachments formed of 21 officers and 388 men.

They wore red serge 'jumpers'(or loose tunics), yellow-ochre cord breeches, dark-blue puttees, and a white pith-helmet. They were equipped with a rifle, sword-bayonet, bandolier of brown leather worn over left shoulder, holding 50 cartridges, brown belt, pouch, frog and sling, haversack and waterbottle; brown ankle boots.

Uniforms

Except at Kirbekan and Ginnis when red coats were worn, the British troops wore khaki throughout the Sudan campaign; shades of khaki varied, perhaps grey for troops from Egypt (many writers and correspondents refer to the force being dressed in grey) and dun for troops from India. Infantry sometimes wore puttees or gaiters, on other occasions the trousers fell 'long' on to the boots. It is possible that the 60th (KRRC) wore a green jacket with red collar, black trousers and a white helmet (there exists a coloured print of El Teb showing this) with all other troops wearing khaki (grey). Highlanders may have had white spats, while puttees could be white (as for Yorks and Lancs), blue, or a darker tan shade. The Royal Artillery wore a blue tunic with red collar and cuffs, khaki helmet with pagri, khaki trousers and blue puttees. Royal Engineers probably wore khaki, although the El Teb print depicts them wearing a red tunic with black collar, blue trousers with red seam stripes, black gaiters and white helmet. Belts and helmet were either buff or white.

The Royal Marines wore a grey/khaki tunic with five brass buttons, trousers without puttees, buff-coloured helmet with pagri; buff waist-belt, cartridges and rifle-strap; white haversack; black boots and black bayonet scabbard with brass tip; blue flash with silver regimental badge on shoulder-straps. The Naval Brigade wore a variety of combinations of blue and white jacket and trousers; straw hat, white round hat or sun helmet. Leggings were either canvas or black leather.

The 10th Hussars wore a khaki uniform and puttees, India helmet with spike and chin-scales; the 19th Hussars wore a blue tunic, blue or khaki trousers and blue puttees; white or khaki helmet without spike. The Mounted Infantry wore full khaki uniform with puttees of a darker shade; some men wore trousers of their original unit, such as trews; light khaki or white helmet with brass spike and badge.

The Expedition's Weapons

From 1871 until the advent of smokeless powder, the British soldier was armed with the Martini-

▲ *Private of the 1st Battalion The Grenadier Guards, Guards Camel Regiment. The sword bayonet was specially issued for the expedition. (Painting by Pierre Turner)*

Henry .45in single-shot rifle, in trained hands accurate to 1,000 yards and more. Battalion volley-fire against massed targets frequently opened at 600 to 800 yards, and even an average marksman could obtain hits at 300 to 400 yards; its soft lead slug was a man-stopper that smashed bone and cartilage and left appalling wounds. With its small bore, greater range, lower trajectory and superior accuracy, it was far in advance of any arm previously issued to the British soldier. With fixed bayonet, the rifle was 5 feet $11\frac{1}{2}$ inches in length ($49\frac{1}{2}$ inches without bayonet) and weighed 9 pounds. At Abu Klea in 1885, the single-shot Martini-Henry, plus some constantly jamming Gardner guns, in the hands of Stewart's 1,000 men strewed 1,100 dead Dervishes around the square in an action that lasted only five minutes.

Gatling and Gardner Guns

The Gatling, an early machine-gun, consisted of a number of very simple breech-loading rifled barrels grouped and revolving about a shaft, with reloading and ejection mechanisms behind; the magazine was

▼ *A Gatling gun, manned by men of the Naval Brigade. The Gatling was prominent in most of the desert battles of the 1884-5 campaign.*

a hopper above the gun from which cartridges dropped by gravity feed. It was hand operated; turning the crank handle at the side rotated the barrels, each of which fired in succession. Its heavy-calibre — .45in — bullet, its high rate of concentrated fire, plus its built-in fearsome 'terror' factor, made it an ideal weapon for colonial wars such as that in the Sudan.

In the mid seventies The Royal Navy chose the Gardner gun to replace the Gatling. The Gardner had five barrels arranged side-by-side. Clips of .45in cartridges were fed vertically into the gun which was operated by cranking a handle. The rate of fire could be up to 120 rounds per minute. Pulled by blue-jackets, the gun was used by the Naval Brigade in the Sudan.

Artillery

The artillery used in the campaign was of an *ad hoc* nature, usually borrowed from the Royal Navy and mounted on land carriages of one kind or another. There were 7pdrs and 9pdrs (actually 6cwt and 8cwt guns, complete with field-carriages and limbers); the 7pdrs were mounted on Egyptian

▲ *Gardner guns manned by Naval Brigade personnel accompanied Graham's Suakim force and Stewart's Desert Column: it is not known whether those seen here are in action at El Teb, Tamai, Abu Klea or Abu Kru.*

▶ *The 7pdr guns were usually mounted on Egyptian Army camel battery carriages; the gun had to have a leather collar fitted around the trunnion so that it would fit on a camel's back.*

camel-battery carriages, with leather collars around the trunnions to make them fit. These were not regarded with much favour because their small calibre and lack of shrapnel shells made them relatively ineffective. In accounts of the battles of 1884-5 7pdr screw-guns are mentioned; these were almost certainly the 2.5in mountain guns so prominent on the frontiers of India. Mention is also made of Krupp guns and bronze guns, both of which were with the disastrous Hicks and Baker Pasha expeditions, and subsequently used against the British, manned by impressed Egyptian artillerymen captured by the Mahdists. Where these guns were used by British forces they were undoubtedly provided from Egypt.

Tactics

In the Sudan British tactics were simple and straightforward, devised to withstand the customary ferocious charges by an enemy who enjoyed numerical superiority; thus there was little room for variation from the advance in densely compact formation, and fighting from hollow squares: either one large square or two smaller squares in echelon, each covering the other's flank. Artillery and machine-guns (i.e., Gatlings and Gardners) were usually sited at the corners of the square where, unavoidably, they were particularly vulnerable to a sudden onrush by the natives; a further complication was their inability to keep pace with the infantry if it charged or was forced back. The

▲ 'On the Road to Metammeh: a British Square' by R. Caton Woodville: this is probably a 7pdr gun (borrowed from the Royal Navy). The Desert Column advanced on Metammeh, so this scene might have been drawn at Abu Klea or the lesser action at Abu Kru.

◄ For static defence and night halts, thorn-bush enclosures were invariably constructed. Those depicted here were situated eight miles from Suakim, and were made either during Graham's operations in early 1884 or at the conclusion of the campaign in March 1885.

at corners of squares, mentioned earlier, and the limitations of a square when mounting an infantry charge from it. At El Teb, the 65th's charge opened up a small gap in the formation; at Tamai, when ordered to charge, the Black Watch responded so enthusiastically that, with the rest of the square stationary, a large gap developed into which, screened by the smoke and dust haze, the natives obligingly rushed.

Zarebas

During periods of static defence and for night halts, zarebas were constructed; these usually consisted of the thorn-bush enclosure peculiar to the Sudan, but sometimes had low mud walls, as at Fort Baker near Suakim. Stationary fortified positions resembling

British fought in line at Kirbekan (Nile Column); at Hashin in the eastern Sudan, and in the later battle of Ginnis — in each case they were on the offensive.

The experiences of Graham's force during the first Suakim campaign reveal a number of cogent aspects, such as the vulnerability of guns positioned

the Roman marching fort, they made it possible to organize supply-points and strongholds on proposed lines of march, protected lines of communication and provided a stronghold on which to fall back.

Mounted Tactics

Cavalry tactics were equally basic, hard experience at El Teb having revealed that the massed charge did not fare too well against loose formations of Sudanese warriors. Here the cavalry made the mistake of charging the Mahdists after they had been repulsed from an attack on a square, but were far from being beaten. The nature of the ground, broken by rocky depressions and thickly strewn with fearsome thorn bushes, prevented a 'knee-to-

knee' charge, so that individual riders found themselves coming up against an agile foe, capable of evasion while delivering a deadly strike, or lying on the ground below the reach of sabres, and slashing at the horses' legs or throwing hardwood 'boomerangs' at them. It was said that the British cavalry when charging the Mahdist foot suffered greater casualties than the enemy; better results were obtained when attacking native horsemen. Subsequently, in an endeavour to solve the problem of killing a prone enemy from horseback, native spears were modified as lances, the head weighted with rolled sheet iron.

So cavalry were used mainly in the scouting role, and to overawe the enemy in retreat and prevent them from re-forming. On occasions cavalry dismounted and, using the carbine, fought as skirmishers, frequently joining with the Mounted Infantry, as did the 10th Hussars at Tamai.

Ad hoc locally raised mounted infantry were usually sent out ahead of the cavalry to make contact with the enemy, their rifles' greater range than that of the carbine making them very effective as scouts and skirmishers.

The Mahdi's Army — the Ansar

From 1880 to 1884 the Mahdi and his disciples united the majority of the nomadic and pastoral tribes who inhabited the extensive arid desert lands south and west of Upper Egypt —the Mahdist army was essentially a collection of regional armies. This great assembly of devoted followers was welded into one army — the Ansar, an Arabic word meaning 'follower' or 'Helper', used in the Koran to describe the disciples of the Prophet Mohammed. The British, Egyptians and Turks knew them as 'Dervishes' or 'Darveesh', a slang term of Persian origin, common throughout the Levant and North Africa to describe itinerant monks and mendicants who regaled the incredulous with popular magical rites and displays in the market-places of those regions.

From the moment when he recruited 311 men from local tribes, armed only with spears and sticks, to rout Abu Su'ud's Egyptian force that had come up the river to Abba, the Mahdi's army multiplied daily. Spreading like wildfire, news of his victory brought tribes flocking to his banner, who lifted him up on a wave of religious adoration and were ready to die for him. They were wild followers but he exacted from them a sense of duty and discipline unknown to the Egyptian soldiers, whom his rapidly growing forces defeated in a number of small engagements. The defeat of Hicks at Shaykan heralded the beginnings of the development of an army that eventually would be capable of tactics and manoeuvres superior to the earlier one-phase frontal attack, and whose use of surprise and natural exploitation of the singular terrain would compensate the heavy losses incurred when attacking in the face of heavy fire. Having seen the effects of such fire during his first abortive attack on El Obeid, the Mahdi rescinded his earlier directive forbidding the use of firearms, and began to arm selected groups with the rifles captured from the Egyptians; the numerous artillery weapons and machine-guns he had taken were put into use, manned by Egyptian gunners captured and cowed into turning their coats.

On 28 December 1881 in a night attack his forces totally destroyed Bashid Bey's 1,300-strong Egyptian column from Fashoda; 8,000 Mahdists advanced in a battle formation resembling an early Islamic array, with rows of infantry just like rows of men at prayer, and horsemen on the wings successfully exploiting an ambush. This victory brought thousands more tribesmen to the Mahdi's base at Qadir, and the organization of units and commands began at this improvised military training camp.

Organization of the Mahdi's Army

Now the army was to be divided into Standards, each under command of a Khalifa, and a tripartite battle formation allowing strategic attacks and tactical deployment was practised:

1. Mounted reconnaissance groups to cut the enemy's supply-lines, bring in information, conduct long-range skirmishing to lower enemy morale, spread propaganda and impede progress by filling-in or poisoning wells.

2. Deployment of up to 50,000 assault warriors armed with swords and spears, supported by cavalry.

3. Deployment of the Jihadiya (riflemen), non-Arab Sudanese from southern Sudan, the Nuba Mountains and Darfur in the far west, armed with breech-loading Remington rifles taken from defeated Egyptians; cartridges carried in locally made leather bandoliers worn around the waist. There were about 7,000 of these soldiers, in units of about twenty men assembled in groups of 'hundreds', led by Amirs. In time they would become the hard core of the new army.

The Mahdist army went through three phases of organization. First as a regional affair when commanders in various parts of the country had to rely on locally raised forces to carry out revolts instigated by the Mahdi's agents.

After the defeat of Hicks in 1883 the Mahdi was able to send reinforcements to other areas; before that the forces fighting around Suakim and the Red

▲ *Infantrymen of the Mahdist army: left, a riverine Arab spearman; right, a Beja warrior armed with sword and shield. Their simple dress indicates that these figures are from early in the campaign, before the adoption of the jibbah. (Painting by Richard Scollins)*

Sea, on the Blue Nile around Sennar or opposing the Nile Column at Kirbekan were all regional commands, differing in both dress and organization. It was not until the fall of Khartoum in 1885 that these regional armies could be fully co-ordinated; before that the core of the army was centred around the Mahdi's headquarters, first in Kordofan, then around Khartoum.

His three chief Khalifas raised their Standards and recruits flocked to them from the regions they represented. Although parading at intervals, they were given no formal training or practice of manoeuvres, but their inherent tactical skill and fighting ability made them formidable warriors.

Under the three Khalifas the forces were divided into 'flags' (*rayya*): Khalifa Abdullah's Black Flag

▲ *Depiction by R. Caton Woodville of a minor skirmish between troopers of the 19th Hussars from either the River or the Desert Column and a party of Hadendowa armed with Remington rifles taken from Hicks or* *Baker's defeated Egyptian forces. On the other hand, these cavalrymen may be 10th or 19th Hussars who served with Graham's Suakim force in early 1884.*

◀ *Any man wounded during the fierce desert battles was in for a very hard time, having to be painfully and laboriously carried with the columns as they made their way across the rough and inhospitable terrain, repeatedly beset by Dervish attackers.*

(*al-rayya-al-zarqa*) was drawn from the west, and was formed of Baggara from Kordofan and Darfur plus most of the black riflemen; the Red Flag (*al-rayya-al-hamra*) of the Khalifa Muhammad al-Sharif was drawn from the riverain peoples north of Khartoum; and the Green Flag (*al-rayya-al-khadra*) of the Khalifa Ali-an-Hilu, recruited Arabs from the Gezira region between the Blue and White Niles, south of Khartoum.

Under the Mahdi's overall control each of the 'flags' was organized into *rubs* (literally 'quarters') of no standard size, usually being of from 800 to 1,200 men. Theoretically the rubs were divided into three combat units and an administrative unit. The first combat unit was formed of spearmen, divided into 'standards' of tribes and sections of tribes; then there were the Jihadiya (regular riflemen) in standards of about 100 men each; and the cavalry,

▶ *This graphic illustration by Caton Woodville is dated 6 September 1884 and must represent Graham's force from Suakim, although their actions at El Teb and Tamai took place much earlier in the year. Wolseley's Relief Expedition did not take the field until the last days of 1884.*

usually Baggara, armed with long spears and swords, but armed with rifles when on reconnaissance or frontier raids. Each standard was subdivided into 'hundreds' under a *ra's mi'a* (head of a hundred - a centurion); and further subdivided into *muqaddamiyya* of 25 men under a *muqaddam*. There were also garrisons of both long-serving regulars living in barracks (usually African riflemen and spear-carrying Arabs) and volunteer recruits from surrounding areas; these formations were organized and subdivided in the same way as the 'flags'.

Amirs led the larger bodies, the smaller sub-units being commanded by local sheiks or *muqqaddamen*. Many of the Amirs wore part armour — cuirasses, mail shirts and shoulder-pieces, high conical helmets with crescent-topped finials and nasal-guards. Mounted on fine Arab horses, their high cantled saddles were richly decorated and the horse's face and rump were covered by fly-fringing. The Amirs were armed with lances and curved swords and they carried metal-studded shields. Those of them who had made the pilgrimage to Mecca wore a green turban.

The Dress of the Ansar

After the fall of El Obeid the Mahdi proclaimed the dress of the Ansar to be: a loose cotton shirt — the *jibbah*, patched originally of necessity but later for decoration; close-fitting cotton drawers or white trousers (*siraval*); sandals (*sayidan*); a girdle of straw

(*karaba*); a skull-cap (*taggia*); a turan (*imma*) with a tail (*ziba*) hanging free behind the left ear; and beads (*sibba*).

The *jibbah*, whose sleeves ended just below the elbows, hung down to the knees. It had symmetrical patches of the same pattern on front and back. Up to 1885 the patches were mostly red and dark-blue, but later, on the familiar 'standard' style of *jibbah*, they could be black, blue or red, occasionally brown, tan or green. They became very 'professionally' made with geometric patches stitched to the front, back and arms, and coloured material edging neck, sleeves and the bottom hem of the garment. Although worn by most of the main army, it was infrequently seen at the battles of 1884-5 where so many warriors were regional levies, few coming from the Mahdi's organized main army.

At Abu Klea and Abu Kru, for example, most of the Ansar wore a white cotton robe wrapped around the waist, with one end tied over the left shoulder; shaved head surmounted by a white cotton skull-cap. At this time some warriors shaved the head and wore a patterned skull-cap and the *jibbah*, and patches on both cap and garment were mostly red or blue — but neither these nor the *jibbah* were of the same shape or decorated in the same way as the later familiar fashion. The more standard style of *jibbah* began to appear at about the time of the Battle of Ginnis (30 December 1885), although there are sketches of this action portraying Ansar warriors wearing a sleeveless *jibbah*.

The Beja, the Bisharin and many Baggara wore ankle-length white cotton trousers, or loin-cloths worn 'dhoti-fashion' around the waist; invariably they were stained by the dust and grime of long usage to drab shades of grey, tan or brick-red. In the early days of the Mahjiyyah they occasionally showed allegiance to the Mahdi by sewing a patch or two in red or blue on to their clothing. They wore their hair long and in elaborate styles, frizzed and stiffened so that it stood out six or eight inches from each side of the head, then parted over each ear and around to the back of the head, the hair below the parting being brushed downwards and outwards, that above the parting upwards; then a long wooden pin or stick was run through the top part of the hair. When the Beja took to wearing the *jibbah* (in later campaigns) they gave up their usual

▲ *A Taaishi warrior of the Baggara tribe.*

costume, shaved the head and wore a skull-cap. There is no record of any distinct tribal hair styles or manner of dress to distinguish the various sections of the Beja, who were the only Mahdists in this period to carry a shield into battle, although not at Abu Klea or Abu Kru.

Just as the Beja wore their normal costume, and the *jibbah* was the short garment worn by the poor and humble of 19th-century Sudan, so most of the Hadendowa and other 'Fuzzie-Wuzzies' of the eastern Sudan did not shave their hair or wear the *jibbah*.

Strictly forbidden, the fez was never worn. Some important Amirs wore a red turban (*imma*) and the style of wearing it was just as much a badge of Mahdism as the *jibbah*, being wrapped around the skull-cap, one end being allowed to hang loose under the folds of the *imma* behind the left ear, the

▼ *Mahdist troops during the later part of the campaign, including a mounted amir and a standard bearer. They now wear the full uniform of the Ansar, including* jibbah, *turbans and sandals. The geometric patches on the* jibbah *are typical, as is the pattern of the standard. (Painting by Richard Scollins)*

remainder being so wrapped that its successive folds formed an inverted 'V' in front, not unlike a Sikh's turban.

The Ansar's Weapons

During the early stages of the revolt the Mahdi's followers were ill-fed and ill-equipped; victories brought more affluent followers and rations improved, while captured Remington rifles supplemented spears, swords and daggers. Most of the Ansar were armed with a 10-foot-long, broad-bladed spear, three shorter throwing spears, a straight, double-edged cross-hilted sword, usually carried in a red leather scabbard hung from the left shoulder under the armpit, close to the body. Most warriors had a short dagger, curved or straight, carried in a red leather sheath fastened to the left

◀ *An R. Caton Woodville depiction of Beja and Hadendowa warriors attacking a British square: almost certainly a hypothetical situation, having been published on 3 January 1885 — too early for the Relief Column's operations, but months after Graham's Battles of El Teb or Tamai.*

upper arm. The Beja and the Bisharin sometimes carried a wicked hooked knife, the blade broadening towards the tip; and a hooked wooden throwing-stick for use against the legs of horses and camels to bring them down. Shields were round with a large conical centre boss, made from rhinoceros, crocodile or elephant hide; they were said to be capable of deflecting a bullet, but were seldom carried except by the Beja. When carried by other tribes shields were of the Baggara type, elliptical with raised centre boss; on occasions rectangular shields of wickerwork were seen. Chain mail was not worn in battle.

It was said that as many as 21,000 rifles together with ammunition were captured from the defeated Egyptian forces. They were mostly the Remington breech-loader, outdated but still a revolutionary weapon for its day when it was produced in 1865; the Egyptian Army adopted it in 1870. Its rolling-block breech made it as simple, strong and foolproof as a gun could be; the breech was opened by cocking the hammer and rolling the solid breech-block back with the thumb so that a cartridge could be inserted. The block was then rolled back up while the hammer was held cocked by a locking lever, then locked the breech closed. When fired, the hammer struck the firing-pin mounted in the breech-block and added its weight to the breech at the moment of explosion. The greater the recoil the more closely the components of the gun interlocked, being so designed that pressure from the chamber forced them more tightly together. It was claimed that the Remington could be fired seventeen times a minute, but its accuracy was greatly impaired by the Dervish habit of shortening the barrel and firing high.

A few percussion muzzle-loaders were in use, and some Martini-Henrys which had found their way into the Sudan. If a Dervish warrior had a rifle, he obtained a bandolier, sometimes two, mostly locally made in coloured stamped leather, but some of captured Egyptian issue; they were worn around the waist or over the shoulder. Firearms were restricted to riflemen although occasionally cavalry on reconnaissance or raiding were issued with a rifle.

The Ansar's heavy equipment was limited to that captured from the Egyptians; from them in the Suakim area in 1884 it is believed that the Arabs acquired 4,000 Remingtons, five Krupp field guns, two Gatlings, two rocket-tubes and an abundance of ammunition. In other engagements they captured some aged brass mountain howitzers mounted on small carriages that were towed by camels; more Krupp guns; some multi-barrelled Nordenfelt machine-guns and some other crank-operated quick-firers. The Arabs also had a handful of old and dilapidated river steamers.

Despite their possession of numerous guns, some of them quite modern, and a variety of machine-guns, with impressed artillerymen trained to man them, the Ansar made little effective use of them. In some cases guns were placed on steamers or defensively in small forts or redoubts; in 1885 such positions along the Nile caused damage to steamers.

Flags

Subdivisions within the army were recognized by their flags, each Amir having his own on which his command mustered; within that command each lesser Amir and *ra's mi'a* (head of a hundred) had his own flag. Banners and flags were rectangular, measuring about four feet by three feet; they were manufactured in Omdurman, and when not in use were stored in the arsenal there. Decorated on one side only, they were embroidered with religious texts, more often than not in four lines, on a white background with coloured borders; although there were flags of solid colours — blue, red or green, with lettering in red, blue, black, green or white. Staffs were embellished with brass balls, flat-topped globes or crescents, some bearing additional decoration such as a horse's tail.

The Ansar's Battle Tactics

In their early days against the Egyptians the Mahdists' tactics were relatively unsophisticated. Taking advantage of the known Egyptian soldiers' habits when halting for the night, of unpacking and building a zareba, without taking such elementary precautions as putting out scouts or vedettes, or manning outposts. Then, waiting until the Egyptians were occupied — drawing water, unloading camels or perhaps just resting after the exertions of the day — the warriors would charge in a dense mass to exploit enemy confusion with speed

▲ *Left, a spearman of the Mahdi's Ansar; right, a Beja warrior. They now wear the* jibbah *and skull-caps in accord with the orders of their leader. (Painting by Richard Scollins)*

and surprise. With broad-bladed spear held up to protect the face (it was also noted that on occasions they hurtled forward with closed eyes) they crashed home; often against a backdrop of women and children beating drums and screaming war-cries. Conversely, the Egyptian habit of encumbering their expeditions with wives and camp followers exacerbated the débâcle that would follow.

The prime factors in Ansar tactics were surprise and shock, often based on encirclement and assaults from two directions, or a surprise attack along the enemy's line of march, sometimes trying to overwhelm the opponent by superior numbers. It was known for riflemen, working themselves into positions close to the enemy, to screen sword and spearmen while softening-up the enemy for the final charge. The assault-warriors made maximum use of cover in getting close to the enemy before launching the attack. The nature of the terrain often allowed the bulk of the warriors to lie undetected among the thorn bushes so that the final charge was the first indication of their presence. Being a natural formation requiring neither drill nor organization, simply because the bravest moved fastest and arrived first, their attacks usually came in wedge-formation which automatically enlarged a breach once its point had penetrated the defence. It was the practice to place the best men in front with some in reserve in order to hit the enemy once they were broken.

This great host of warriors would suddenly and dramatically rise from the scrub or a depression in the ground, a black cloud moving forward at an incredible pace, seemingly reaching the speed of galloping horses. Their large phalanxes were each headed by a superbly mounted Amir, attended by his standard-bearer and attendants. As the host jogged forward their momentum kept time with the drums beating incessantly in their rear; standing in the stirrups, the Amirs waved them on, boosting their fervour with shouted Islamic slogans and prayers.

The Ansar was also capable of making long approach marches at great speed, the foot warriors keeping up with those mounted on hardy camels and horses — a gift of mobility they used to good effect. On the march and in battle signals were given by drums and horns.

GRAHAM'S FIRST CAMPAIGN FROM SUAKIM

On 29 February 1884 Graham's force marched out of Trinkatat; the infantry in square formation with Mounted Infantry ahead, a squadron of 10th Hussars covering the front and the remainder of the cavalry in rear. The front face of the square was formed by the Gordons, the rear by The Black Watch — both marching in company columns of fours at company intervals. With Royal Engineers in support, at the left-hand angle of the front face were two Gatlings and one Gardner, at the right one Gatling and two Gardners; there were four 7pdrs of the RA at each angle of the rear face. On the right flank marched the 89th with part of the four companies of the KRRC on line and the rest in quarter-column support; the 65th in line on the left flank with the RMLI in quarter-column support. The flanks marched in open company columns with guns in the intervals at the angles; transport camels with ammunition and medical supplies were in the centre of the formation.

The Battle of El Teb

On learning of the landing of Graham's force, Osman Digna sent his nephew Madani ibn Ali to reinforce Abdallah ibn Hasid, the Amir of the coast, and together they fortified an abandoned sugar refinery near Baker's old battlefield of El Teb. Here they had some 6,000 men, four Krupp guns, two bronze guns and a Gatling; some riflemen were armed with captured Remingtons, mostly in the first skirmish of the battle. The Mahdist force was drawn from the Hadendowa, Senilab, Ashraf, Arteiga and Hassanab, about 2,500-3,000 foot warriors being involved in the main assault.

The huge British square plodded over the hot and barren sandy soil until they came upon the enemy at El Teb, close to the decomposing heaps of mutilated bodies of Baker's defeated army; the Mahdists were behind shallow earthworks, in rifle-

▲ *Admiral Sir William Hewitt, RN, was the commander at Suakim during the early months of 1884. From the fleet stationed there and from passing troopships, he* *assembled a force which General Graham led to victories at El Teb and Tamai.*

pits and a fortified building in front of the village and wells of El Teb. Bugles sounded the advance and bagpipes wailed as Graham marched his square to the right, in an attempt to turn the enemy's left; slowly the formation marched forward for about 1,000 yards under fire of the guns captured from Baker Pasha's expedition, served by artillerymen

◀ Top: This sketch of the Battle of El Teb was drawn by Melton Prior who was present in the British square. It was sent to London on the evening of the battle and arrived on 10 March, having taken little more than ten days to make the long journey from Trinkatat; it was photographed and printed in time for publication five days later.

◀ Below: The Battle of El Teb, 29 February 1884. Detail from a drawing by R. Caton Woodville dated 11 March and published on 15 March. Reaching British breakfast tables soon after it all happened, it depicts a fierce if rather balletic charge of Hadendowa warriors of Osman Digna's army.

▲ The Battle of El Teb. An irresistible headlong charge drove the Yorks and Lancs Regiment back some 30-40 yards before the Arabs driven back in hand-to-hand fighting and the merciless fire from the Naval Brigade's Gatling guns.

treated. It did not take long for the artillery and the rattling Gardners and Gatlings to silence the Krupp guns by driving their gunners away. Now the square rose to its feet and moved forward with the left-face as the front, the Yorks and Lancs supported by the RMLI in the fighting line, with the Gordons and The Black Watch on either flank; the KRRC and the Royal Irish were in the rear. The infantry advanced in a shoulder-to-shoulder wheeling movement, without losing cohesion, towards the enemy's left flank.

In scattered cover, about 2,000 of the Ansar were spread out along their front, and large groups hovered on the flanks of the square. As they advanced, Graham's infantry fired first volleys and them independently, but it was not enough to stop the natives who, when only about 200 yards separated the forces, charged in a headlong rush, waving their broad-bladed spears and cross-hilted swords. The Yorks and Lancs fell back about 30-40 yards, opening a gap in the British formation into which some of the enemy rushed, to be dispatched by Marines moving up in support. A second charge came into the square on all sides, and the flanks

captured at the fall of Tokar and impressed into the Mahdi's service. The square halted and Graham brought his guns into action at about 900 yards' range; it was noon and very hot so the infantry were ordered to lie down while casualties were being

The Battle of El Teb, 29 February 1884

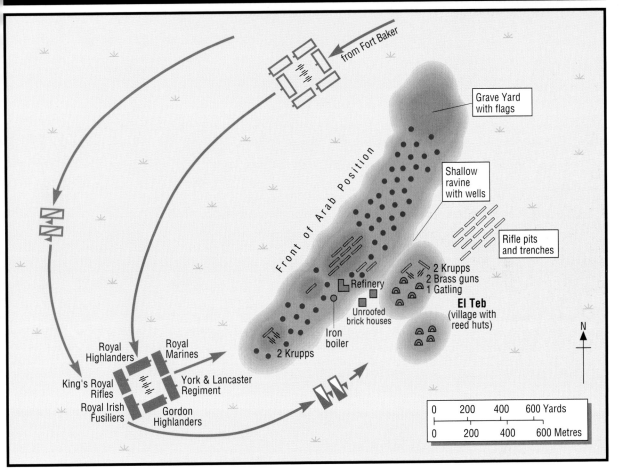

from Fort Baker

Grave Yard
with flags

Front of Arab Position

Shallow
ravine
with wells

Rifle pits
and trenches

2 Krupps
2 Brass guns
1 Gatling

Refinery

Unroofed
brick houses

El Teb
(village with
reed huts)

Iron
boiler

2 Krupps

Royal
Highlanders

Royal
Marines

King's Royal
Rifles

York & Lancaster
Regiment

Royal Irish
Fusiliers

Gordon
Highlanders

N

0	200	400	600 Yards

0	200	400	600 Metres

◀ El Teb. The Ansar warriors entrenched themselves in earthworks and a fortified sugar-refinery from which Krupp field guns (captured from Baker Pasha) caused casualties among the 65th and Gordon Highlanders advancing in attack.

◀ The Battle of El Teb fought on 29 February by Graham's force out of Suakim, saw the British cavalry, charging over rough and difficult terrain, roughly handled by Dervish warriors who lay on the parched earth and hacked at the horses' legs.

handled a double-barrelled 12 bore shotgun loaded with pig-shot, bringing down onrushing natives like driven hares. The second charge repulsed, the Yorks and Lancs and the Marines rushed the redoubt to their front, carrying it with the guns it contained.

Now the Sudanese withdrew steadily and in good order to their prepared positions in and around the refinery and in the village. Mistaking the withdrawal for a retreat, Stewart sent in all his cavalry, but the broken ground and thick bush prevented a knee-to-knee charge and, to the cavalry's surprise, the natives held their ground, dropping to the parched earth as the cavalrymen rode at them, and attempting to hamstring the horses and throwing boomerangs of mimosa-wood at their legs. At one point thirty Arab horsemen, riding bareback and wielding large two-edged swords, charged an entire squadron and caused casualties before being wiped

were briefly engaged in hand-to-hand fighting with this savage enemy which attacked like a swarm of furious bees, throwing themselves on to levelled bayonets and falling in dozens from the close-range massed fire of dozens of Martini-Henry rifles. Positioned outside the square, Fred Burnaby of The Blues (out in the desert 'on sick leave') deftly

▲ *Battle of El Teb: the 42nd Regiment (The Black Watch) assault the fortified Arab positions.*

out. The British cavalry found the Arabs on the ground to be out of sabre reach, and later Stewart had native spears adapted to serve as lances, the heads weighted with rolled sheet iron.

On the left of the Ansar position around the refinery and wells, the infantry advanced on the enemy's rear, the RMA manning the Krupps and bronze guns and turning them on the tenacious Arabs holding the sugar mill and the rifle-pits. The Gordons and the Naval Landing Party played an outstanding part in these last stages when every inch of ground was contested by the warriors who sprang out of the ground like rabbits.

By 2 p.m. the battle was over; the Ansar withdrawing sullenly, leaving about 1,500 dead on the field and about the same number wounded. The dead included the Amirs Abdallah ibn Hasid, Madani ibn Ali, al-Tihar ibn al-Hajj, Una Gamar al-Din al-Majdhub and Musa Qilay. Following the battle there were no significant defections or desertions from Osman Digna's force. Graham sustained the following casualties shown in the table. This list is taken from C. B. Norman's book

published in 1911 and seems remarkably low; other sources give 34 killed and 155 wounded; 30 killed and 142 wounded. Leaving the Black Watch at El Teb, Graham's force marched on to Tokar which they reached on 3 March; they picked up some survivors there and returned to Suakim on the 5th.

Graham's casualties at El Teb

	Officers		Men	
	K	W	K	W
10th Hussars	2	1	4	–
19th Hussars	1	2	13	20
Royal Artillery	–	1	1	–
Naval Brigade	1	2	2	9
Royal Marines	–	2	3	–
Royal Engineers	–	1	1	–
Black Watch	–	3	3	–
Yorks and Lancs	–	3	7	–
Gordon Highlanders	–	–	–	–
KRRC	1	–	–	–
Royal Irish Fusiliers	–	1	–	7

▲ *Native scouts of Graham's Column en route to Tokar after the Battle of El Teb; they appear to be taking advantage of the close proximity of the Nile.*

▼ *After defeating the Mahdists at El Teb on 29 February, General Sir Gerald Graham's force marched on Tokar which had surrendered to Osman Digna on 8 February. Reaching Tokar on 3 March, the force picked up survivors and returned to Suakim.*

The Battle of Tamai

On 10 March, having learned that a strong enemy force was assembled at Tamai, sixteen miles southwest of Suakim, Graham sent The Black Watch (623 officers and men) to secure a zareba site $8^1/2$ miles out of Suakim on the Sinkat road. In the evening of the following day the remainder of the force, plus a new battery of Royal Naval 9pdrs, joined them. On 12 March they marched out in two squares surrounded by cavalry scouts. The guns and Royal Engineers were in a 25-pace interval between

the regiments, forming the front face of each square; as at El Teb, the guns were hauled with ropes by the Naval Brigade. Next morning the force

◀ *On 10 March The Black Watch were sent out by General Graham to secure a zareba $8^1/2$ miles out of Suakim on the Sinkat road. They were joined by the remainder of the force on the evening of the 11th.*

▼ *A fine panorama of the Battle of Tamai, drawn by Melton Prior who is depicted in the forefront of the action accompanied by Mr Cameron, a war correspondent, later killed at Abu Klea.*

set out, again in two squares in echelon from the left, with Davis's 2 Brigade leading and Buller's 1 Brigade on its right rear. Each square had a 200-yard front and a 100-yard flank, and the formations were about 600-900 yards apart. There were cavalry sections in front, the remainder of the cavalry being echeloned to the left-rear of 2 Brigade. The composition and strength of the force was much the same as at El Teb, plus the new RA battery. Also there were 66 camels bearing 96 rounds per gun, and 107 Egyptian artillerymen as camel-leaders; the Scottish Divisional RA had 52 mules carrying 86 rounds per gun.

It was thought that the Ansar forces, commanded by Osman Digna's cousin, Mahsud Musa, were about 9-12,000 strong, some in a large ravine, others hidden in bushes to the right of the British squares; they included only about 150 riflemen, untrained and ineffective. The entire force was out of sight of

the British cavalry and Graham's Abyssinian scouts, and when the leading square was some 200 yards from the ravine it was suddenly assailed by large numbers of tribesmen in a series of fierce rushes. Frantically the infantry opened fire, but despite bugle calls and orders could not be persuaded to aim steadily or reserve fire, so that dense clouds of smoke hung in the still air which enabled the enemy to creep closer unseen.

Sent to charge the ravine, The Black Watch advanced, firing independently to right and left when thirty yards from the cleft; although ordered not to do so, some of the 65th followed the Highlanders, causing a gap to open up in the face of the square and leaving the Gatlings and Gardners outside the formation. Under cover of the smoke, large groups of the enemy burst from the haze, hitting The Black Watch in the flank and causing the guns to be abandoned — the Naval Brigade

locked the Gatlings and Gardners before leaving them; the Marines were hit and the square was sent reeling back about 800 yards to the east. Small groups fighting back-to-back, disputed every inch of the ground, gradually checking the withdrawal, until rallied and re-formed by the officers and NCOs.

Five hundred yards away to the right-rear Buller's square was being attacked in the same furious manner, but blew away the approaching enemy by sheer weight of firepower; they then switched their fire to the tribesmen attacking Davis's square. At the same time, the cavalry galloped round to the left flank of the square, dismounted and opened fire with carbines, catching the attackers in a crossfire. After about twenty minutes the attacks had been repulsed and 2 Brigade re-formed with Marines on the right, 65th in the centre and Black Watch on the left; the Naval

Brigade formed in their rear. After halting for about fifteen minutes, Graham moved his force forward, 1 Brigade on the right firing at close range and retaking lost ground and abandoned guns; the enemy had dumped one gun down the ravine and set an ammunition-limber on fire. Then 2 Brigade turned their machine-guns on the enemy in the ravine and drove them out; moving amid wounded tribesmen lying in the thick scrub, who fired or slashed at any one within reach, 2 Brigade took a ridge above the village of Tamai and the battle

▼ *The Battle of Tamai, 13 March 1884. When a gap was forced in the face of the British square, leaving the Gatling and Gardner guns outside the formation, the Dervishes rushed in so quickly that* *the guns had to be abandoned. This drawing by on-the-spot artist, Melton Prior, depicts their recapture.*

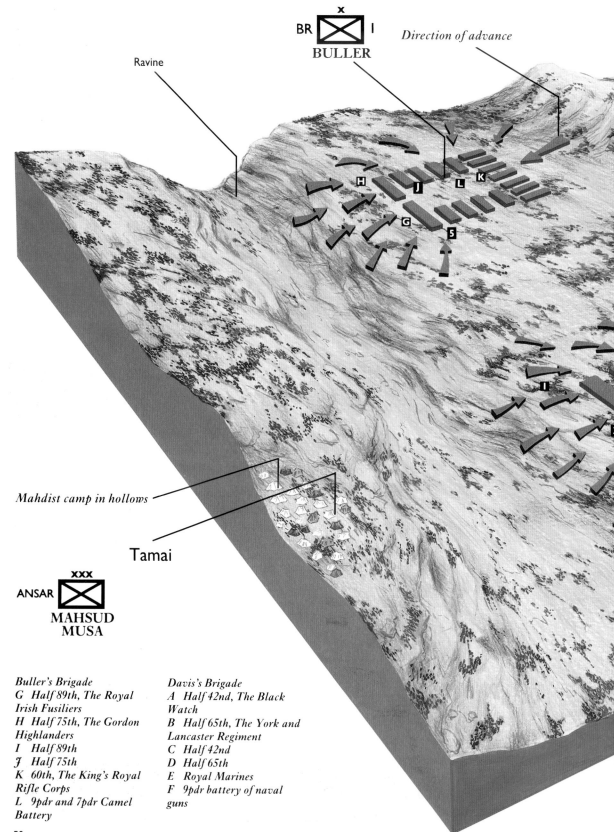

BR **BULLER** I

Direction of advance

Ravine

H J L K

G 5

II

E

Mahdist camp in hollows

Tamai

ANSAR **MAHSUD MUSA**

Buller's Brigade
G   Half 89th, The Royal
Irish Fusiliers
H   Half 75th, The Gordon
Highlanders
I   Half 89th
J   Half 75th
K   60th, The King's Royal
Rifle Corps
L   9pdr and 7pdr Camel
Battery

Davis's Brigade
A   Half 42nd, The Black
Watch
B   Half 65th, The York and
Lancaster Regiment
C   Half 42nd
D   Half 65th
E   Royal Marines
F   9pdr battery of naval
guns

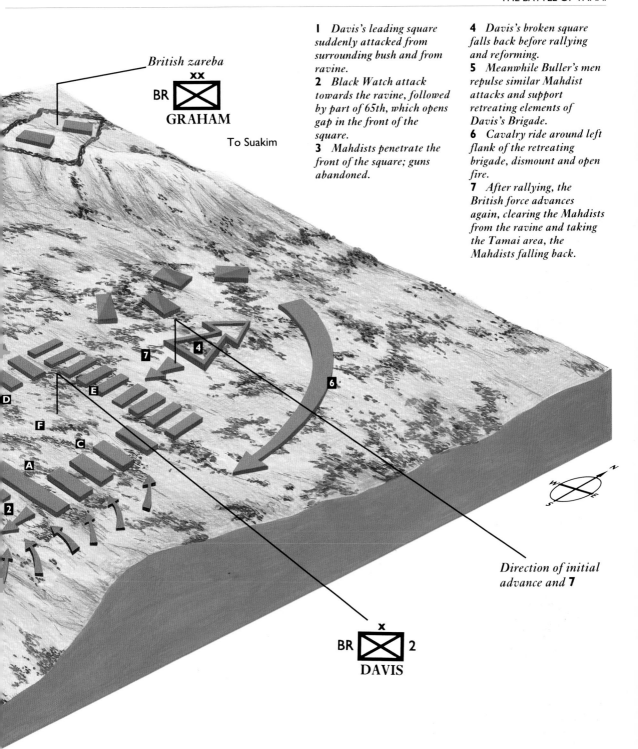

British zareba

BR **XX** GRAHAM

To Suakim

1 Davis's leading square suddenly attacked from surrounding bush and from ravine.
2 Black Watch attack towards the ravine, followed by part of 65th, which opens gap in the front of the square.
3 Mahdists penetrate the front of the square; guns abandoned.

4 Davis's broken square falls back before rallying and reforming.
5 Meanwhile Buller's men repulse similar Mahdist attacks and support retreating elements of Davis's Brigade.
6 Cavalry ride around left flank of the retreating brigade, dismount and open fire.
7 After rallying, the British force advances again, clearing the Mahdists from the ravine and taking the Tamai area, the Mahdists falling back.

Direction of initial advance and 7

BR **x** 2 DAVIS

THE BATTLE OF TAMAI

13 March 1884, as seen from the south-east

petered out. Graham's casualties were as shown to the right, while the Ansar suffered about 2,000 killed and the same number wounded.

At both El Teb and Tamai the British had been left in possession of the field, but the Mahdists had withdrawn slowly and in good order on both occasions. Subsequently, an historian of the Mahdiyya was to write: 'British intervention had proved practically ineffectual. Osman Digna retained both Sinkat and Tokar and the Suakim-Berber route was controlled by the Ansar.' On 28 March, after several abortive skirmishes, Graham received orders to close the campaign. Leaving two British battalions to garrison Suakim, Graham embarked the remainder of his force on 3 April and sailed for Egypt.

It is not unreasonable to say that very little of practical value was achieved through these two pyrrhic victories.

A medal and a clasp were granted for these actions, and the battle honour 'Egypt 1884' was granted to the 10th and 19th Hussars, The Black Watch, York and Lancaster Regiment and the Gordon Highlanders.

Graham's casualties at Tamai				
	Officers		Men	
	K	W	K	W
Black Watch	1	4	60	29
65th	1	1	30	23
Gordons	–	1	1	8
KRRC	–	–	–	5
Royal Irish Fusiliers	–	1	–	5
Royal Marines	–	–	3	15
Naval Brigade	3	–	6	7

◀ *Major General Charles George Gordon, CB, in his uniform as Governor General of the Sudan, as portrayed in* **The Illustrated London News** *in March 1884.*

KHARTOUM

In the early 1880s Khartoum was the capital of the Sudan, an Egyptian colony since the 1820s. It had a mixed population of about 50,000 of whom perhaps 30,000 were slaves. There was a wealthy class of Egyptian merchants and officials, and a mixed bunch of Europeans — Greeks, Austrians, Italians, some British, a few Indians, Jews, Syrians, Algerians and Abyssinians. The principal route to the outside world was the River Nile which linked the Sudan with Cairo. On 10 February, before reaching Khartoum, Gordon had sent the Mahdi a red robe of honour and a fez, accompanied by a letter offering him the Sultanate of Kordofan; in a letter received on 22 March, the Mahdi refused the offer and returned the clothing. He enclosed a Mahdist *jibbah*, inviting Gordon to become a follower of the Mahdiyya. This incident, revealing to Gordon that he had underestimated the Mahdi's convictions,

▶ *It is known from his journals that Gordon, during the siege of Khartoum, spent much time on the roof of his palace, scanning the empty waters of the Nile for signs of a relieving force.*

▲ Lieutenant of the King's Royal Rifle Corps Mounted Infantry Camel Regiment, 1884–5. (Painting by Pierre Turner)

plus what his eyes had told him en route to Khartoum, radically changed Gordon's concept of his mission.

Although on arrival he had energetically begun plans for the disciplined withdrawal envisaged and expected by the respective governments in London and Cairo, his spies told him that it would be extremely difficult if not impossible to bring this about. Now it seemed to him that his primary aim should be the establishment of a rival government to that of the Mahdi. At this stage still in reasonable communication with Cairo and, through the British Agent, with London, Gordon suggested that Zobeir be appointed Governor-General of the Sudan, but was turned down. He next proposed the delaying of the evacuation and the dispatch of British and Indian troops to Wadi Halfa and Berber, claiming that the Mahdi could be smashed by an expedition of reasonable size. He backed this by stating his conviction that unless the Mahdi were defeated now, even an evacuation to Egypt would only postpone the inevitable day when a British force would have to take on the task. Gladstone and his government in London rejected these plans and suggestions.

Left to his own devices, the telegraph line from Cairo having been cut on 13 March, Gordon was now under blockade as the Mahdi raised local tribes and sent a force to put the city under close siege; by mid-May all the territory around Khartoum was in the hands of the Mahdists. By now Gordon had clearly realized that there were no political alternatives to an evacuation and that, with news of the fall of Berber, only a military solution was possible. Either he must defeat the Mahdi himself, or hold Khartoum at all costs until the British government decided to send a major military expedition in relief.

The military resources at his disposal consisted of a garrison of about 2,500 Regular Egyptian and Sudanese troops plus about 5,000 irregulars, for the most part armed with the Remington rifle. There were two Krupp 20pdrs, eleven 7pdr brass mountain-guns, and ten other small guns and howitzers of various sorts and weights; there were also a few Gardner and Nordenfelt machine-guns. There were ample supplies of ammunition.

Khartoum was not wholly unprotected, being shielded on the northern and western sides by the

Blue and White Niles respectively; and on the southern and eastern sides by a line of fortifications stretching from river to river. They had been designed and constructed by Abd el Kader Pasha, the energetic governor-general who had replaced the ineffectual Raouf Pasha in the spring of 1882. When news came of the Arab rebellion in Egypt and more recent Mahdist victories in the Sudan, Gordon lost no time in strengthening the defences of Khartoum. His line of fortification, about a mile from the town, described an arc that protected the town to the east and south, and consisted of a ditch and parapet, with bastions at intervals. Unfortunately the line was far too long to be effectively held by the troops at his disposal, and there was no time to form a new line nearer the town, so Gordon was forced to devote the garrison's energy to improving it. Eventually it consisted of a continuous ditch and rampart from the Blue to the White Niles with four 'forts' improvised from fortified houses surrounded by a rampart and ditch. As would Baden-Powell at Mafeking years later, Gordon took a delight in improvising unorthodox defences such as 20pdr Krupp shells laid as land-mines, singly or in groups, and fired by fuzes; crows'-feet, wire entanglements, broken bottles, sharpened iron stakes, and buried biscuit boxes filled with nails, bullets and broken glass, set off by pressure or fuzes.

All in all, given the limited means available, the defensive system at Khartoum was well organized and the guns were distributed to their best advantage — so much so that the Mahdists were deterred from mounting an assault until the treacherous Nile opened an easy path for them.

The Gordon Relief Expedition

Concerned by the news that the noose was inexorably tightening around Gordon's neck, British public opinion was hardening against the intractable Gladstone and his government; finally they were forced reluctantly to submit to demands that a relief column be sent to get Gordon out of Khartoum. On 5 August 1884 Parliament authorized funds for the formation of an expedition, to be commanded by General Sir Garnet Wolseley. He arrived in Cairo on 9 September and began organizing his forces. Gordon received news of the expedition on 20 September.

The units making up this all-British force were sent to Egypt from Britain and India, and from garrisons at Gibraltar and Malta. Those in England mobilized at Aldershot, sailed from Portsmouth to Alexandria and took the new railway to Cairo where

▼ *The Camel Regiments parade before their commander, General Sir Herbert Stewart, prior to leaving Korti on 30 December 1884.*

they arrived in early October; at this stage the Camel Regiments were formed and men were taught to ride the ungainly beasts. Eventually the Guards and Light Infantry Camel Regiments, with detachments of the South Staffordshire Regiment and Royal Engineers, were sent to Korti and established a camp on the banks of the Nile, under command of General Sir Herbert Stewart. On 16 December Wolseley reached the camp and, until the end of the month, units arrived daily by land or up the river.

Canadian Voyageurs on the Nile

Wolseley's most pressing problem was how to get about 7,000 men and a huge amount of stores up the Nile to Khartoum which lies 1,629 miles from Cairo, the journey to be made via Wadi Halfa 793 miles south of Cairo, then via Dongola, about another 450 miles. From the second cataract (which is nine miles long) at Wadi Halfa, there are at least six major cataracts and a number of lesser ones. The relatively easy journey as far as the second cataract was made in a large fleet of Nile paddle-steamers, contracted to carry and/or tow Wolseley's army until they would be forced to resort to other forms of water transport to take them to the forward base camp at Korti. With his Red River Expedition of some ten years earlier in mind, Wolseley believed that the troops and stores could ascend the Nile in small sail- and man-powered whale-boats, manned by a contingent of experienced river-men — Canadian Voyageurs — and 386 of them were recruited in Canada and duly arrived in Egypt. Dressed in dark-grey woollen-tweed Norfolk jackets, blue flannel shirts, grey trousers, half-moccasins and white foreign-service helmets, one Voyageur was assigned to take the rudder of each boat.

In late August 1884 orders were placed with 47 British firms for the construction of at least 800 'whaling gigs'; the first 400 had passed acceptance trials and were ready by early September. Although not identical, the boats were generally 30 feet long with a beam of 6 feet 6 inches. Of wooden construction (fir or white pine), each had a deadweight of 600-700 pounds and could carry ten fully equipped soldiers plus its crew of two sailors

or one sailor and a Voyageur. Like beads on a string, they were towed upstream to Wadi Halfa by paddle-steamers chartered from Thomas Cook, being hauled through particularly rough stretches of the Nile by labour gangs of Kroomen, Sudanese natives and Egyptian soldiers. Under sail, the whale-boats were capable of about 6 knots in a light breeze; otherwise six of the men had to row. The Royal Irish Regiment won General Wolseley's prize of £100 for the battalion making the fastest passage from the second cataract to Korti. At the second cataract and in rough water the smaller steamers were manhandled by vast gangs of natives using steel hawsers slung under the hulls.

Wolseley sets his Force in Motion

The hot season was approaching and Gordon was known to be hanging on by the skin of his teeth, so Wolseley planned a campaign that involved dividing his strike force. A mobile Desert Column mounted on camels would cross the Bayuda Desert to Metammeh, occupy the oases of Gakdul and Abu Klea en route, and establish contact with Gordon's steamers at the end of its march. A River Column would fight its way up the Nile, capture Abu Hamed, open up the desert route to Korosko as an additional line-of-communication, drive the rebels from Berber, and join hands with the Desert

▲ The Desert Column set out from Korti on 30 December 1884. R. Caton Woodville depicts native guides and a section of Mounted Infantry at the head of the column.

Column at Metammeh. On 30 December 1884 Sir Herbert Stewart set out from Korti at the head of the Desert Column which consisted of the forces shown in the table overleaf, in all about 1,100 officers and men. They made such good progress that the Column arrived at the Wells of Gakdul on 2 January 1885, having covered 100 miles, and were halfway across the Bayuda Desert. Leaving the Camel Regiment and Royal Engineers at Gakdul,

Stewart's Desert Column

	Officers	Men
Guards Camel Regiment	19	395
Heavy Camel Regiment	24	376
Mounted Infantry Camel Regiment	24	359
1st Bn 35th (Royal Sussex Regiment)	8	250
19th Hussars (2 horsed squadrons)	8	127
26th Coy Royal Engineers($^1/_2$ coy)	2	25
1/1 Southern Divisional RA ($^1/_2$ bty)	4	34
(three 2.5in rifled muzzle-loading screw-guns)		
Naval Brigade (one Gardner)	5	53

Stewart returned to Korti with the remainder of the force to bring back to Gakdul the supplies it was necessary to accumulate there. He left Korti again on 8 January with about 2,000 officers and men, and arrived at Gakdul on 12 January accompanied by Sir Charles Wilson, the Intelligence Officer.

Meanwhile The Black Watch had arrived at Korti on 1 January, and on the 3rd General Earle, commander of the River Column, marched out to join an advance guard of his force which was to take the long route up-river in the steamers and whale-boats. On 5 January, riding a small white donkey, Captain Lord Charles Beresford, RN arrived at Korti with the 1st Division of the Naval Brigade, bringing a Gardner gun. On 14 January Stewart resumed his march towards the oasis of Abu Klea, and on the 16th he was bivouacked within three miles of the wells, having covered the more than forty miles from Gakdul in two days.

The Battle of Abu Klea

Cavalry scouts having reported the presence of the Ansar in strength between them and the wells at Abu Klea, the force built a strong zareba which came under continuous fire throughout the hours of

◄ Top: The Desert Column on their way to Gakdul. The artist Melton Prior portrays himself riding a horse alongside the Camel Regiments; next to him is Mr Cameron, **The Standard**'s war-correspondent who was later killed at the Battle of Abu Klea.

◄ Below: Approaching the wells at Abu Klea, the Desert Column's cavalry scouts sight the enemy. General Stewart goes forward to assess the situation.

▲ Private of the 1st Battalion the York and Lancaster Regiment. (Painting by Pierre Turner)

◀ *R. Caton Woodville's depiction of the Desert Column in the Bayuda Desert in January 1885 when the Battles of Abu Klea and Abu Kru were fought. General Stewart is using his binoculars, the scouting 19th Hussars having reported the enemy's presence and been recalled to the now halted main body.*

darkness, to the accompaniment of persistent throbbing of tom-toms. At reveille, before dawn, the men were stood-to, and were then ordered to disassemble their Martini-Henry rifles and clean the oil from the breech-blocks before polishing them with black lead to prevent sand sticking to the oil and clogging the action. Water was running short and it was essential that they reach the wells as soon as possible. Stewart believed that the enemy was intent on slowing him down, and the only way to counter this and secure the precious water was to vacate the safety of the zareba and march out seeking action.

At 10 a.m., leaving a small garrison in the zareba to protect the baggage, the force began to advance in a huge square over rough and uneven ground; it was very hot. The front face of the square was formed of the Guards Camel Regiment and the Mounted Infantry Camel Regiment which also formed the forward halves of the left and right faces; the Heavy Camel Regiment — No. 5 Company, 5th and 6th Lancers —formed the rear of the left half-face. No. 4 Company, Scots Greys and 1st Royal Dragoon Guards, No. 3 Company, 5th Dragoon Guards, 4th Dragoon Guards, some men from the Naval Brigade, No. 2 Company, Royal Horse Guards, The Bays and No. 1 Company, 1st and 2nd Life Guards, Royal Marines and the Sussex Regiment formed the right face, with the Sussex forming the rear half.

The troops were formed in four ranks with the three 2.5in (7pdr) screw-guns in the centre; there were about 350 men in the front face; 300 on the right and on the left; with another 300 forming the rear. The Naval Brigade's Gardner was in rear of the camels, near the left corner of the square. Some additional Mounted Infantry were thrown out as dismounted skirmishers.

The force moved slowly up a slight rise with a hard gravelled surface, halting occasionally to allow doctors to attend the men wounded by increasing rifle-fire, and to adjust the square whose rear face was being bowed outwards by restive camels. Reaching a point about 200 yards from where numerous Ansar banners stretched across the line-of-march, the square halted for a final re-dressing of the faces. At that moment the banners stirred and a

▼ *The Battle of Abu Klea, 17 January 1885. The Desert Column fought the battle while moving in a huge square which was suddenly attacked by a large Ansar force. The Arabs came to close-quarters when the Naval Gardner gun at the square's left-rear corner jammed, and fierce hand-to-hand fighting took place.*

great host of Dervishes rose into view. Suddenly and dramatically the hot air was alive with shouts, screams and the beating of drums rising above the staccato firing and the hiss of bullets. Then the clamour died away, to be replaced by the crackle of independent firing from the British Martini-Henrys as the huge enemy mass came forward in a serrated line of large phalanxes, each led by a resplendent Amir surrounded by standard-bearer and attendants.

The dark mass jogged forward, the furious drumming of sandalled feet causing the ground to quiver, blending with the repetitious beat of the tom-toms, adding momentum to a pace that soon matched the speed of a galloping horse. Despite the fierce fire poured into the dense mass, they did not falter; natives bleeding from multiple wounds continued their surge forward, others bounded back to their feet having been knocked over by a bullet's impact.

When within about 80 yards of the front face of the square, the enemy ranks began to show signs of the terrible punishment they were taking, great gaps appearing as the rapid and disciplined fire from the four ranks of Guardsmen and Mounted Infantry took effect. Suddenly, and involuntarily, a large section of the charging Dervishes changed direction, swinging to their right around the front left corner of the square towards its rear, where the left face sloped back to give a field of fire to the Naval Gardner which had been run out. After noisily firing a few rounds the gun jammed; sailors, desperately trying to clear it, were enveloped in a cloud of warriors who hacked and slashed at the handful of bluejackets. Lord Charles Beresford, involved in the mêlée, was knocked to the ground but was not injured. Still outside the square and unable to see the attack around the left-face, the skirmishers were masking the fire of their comrades from that area; realizing their danger, Colonel Burnaby of The Blues attempted to bring 3rd Company, Heavy Camel Regiment to their aid, himself riding outside the square. His horse brought down, Burnaby fought furiously with his

▼*Abu Klea. A soldier from a face of the square goes to the aid of a comrade, wounded and left outside the formation.*

The Battle of Abu Klea, 17 January 1885

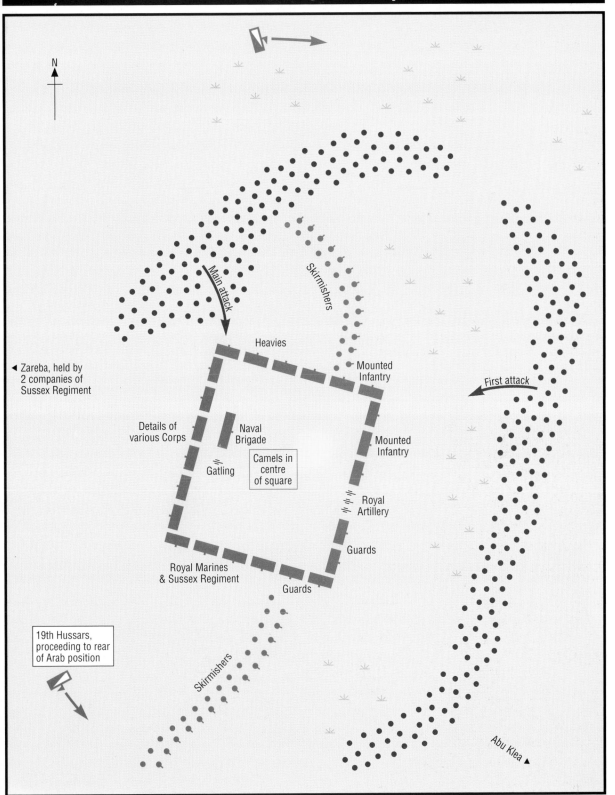

N

Main attack

Skirmishers

Heavies

Mounted
Infantry

First attack

◄ Zareba, held by
2 companies of
Sussex Regiment

Details of
various Corps

Naval
Brigade

Mounted
Infantry

Gatling

Camels in
centre
of square

Royal
Artillery

Guards

Royal Marines
& Sussex Regiment

Guards

19th Hussars,
proceeding to rear
of Arab position

Skirmishers

Abu Klea ▲

▲ *Lieutenant-Colonel Fred Burnaby, commanding officer of The Blues, had taken sick leave in order to join Wolseley in the Sudan.*

He was killed at Abu Klea. The archetypal Victorian soldier, his exploits in foreign wars were legendary.

sword against overwhelming numbers but was cut down and killed — as were most of the skirmishers.

By this time the continuous firing had caused many rifles to overheat and jam, leaving the men to fight with frequently bending bayonets, and rifle butts. Instinctively racing into the gap where the Gardner had stood, Dervishes rushed wildly at the restive camels in the square's centre. Their leader, Abu Saleh, planted his Standard in the midst of the confusion and was almost immediately killed. The right-face units —Royals, Greys and 5th Lancers — were attacked in rear as the front-face's rear units about-faced and, being on higher ground, were able to bring fire to bear over the camels on the attackers. With the left face of the square gradually being forced back towards the front face, and the rear face being pushed in, the camels formed a living traverse which broke the Arabs' rush and gave the defenders time to re-form. Amid a

maelstrom of wildly plunging camels and horses, a slashing, hacking mass of men surged convulsively. General Stewart was unhorsed but unhurt as the enemy began to waver; then the attack ceased as suddenly as it had begun, the drums silenced as though on a signal. Most of the surviving Dervishes with great dignity turned their back on the square and walked slowly away, leaving great piles of their dead behind them.

When no further major attacks came in — there were desultory skirmishes around the fringes of the square as groups of wounded natives, having feigned death, sprang to their feet and lunged at the nearest soldiers — a breathless cheer rippled round the ranks. Quickly Stewart ordered the square to re-form and move on to slightly higher ground. When all was quiet parties of men left the ranks and foraged for waterskins and ammunition from the dead camels. Then the roll was called — nine officers and 72 other ranks had been killed; eight officers and 112 other ranks wounded. The unit breakdown was:as shown below.

In an action lasting about five minutes, it was said that about 1,100 dead Dervishes strewed the ground in the vicinity of the square, from a total force estimated at about 11,500 comprising 2,000 Ababdeh, Bisharin and other Arabs from Berber under the nephew of the Amir of Berber, Abd el Majid; 2,000 Arabs from Metammeh under Ali wad Saad, Amir of Metammeh; 1,000 men from the Mahdi's 'own' army — with 400 rifles; 4-6,000 Kordofan Arabs under Sheik Musa, Amir of the Hamr Arabs; plus a force of 60 soldiers of the old Egyptian army from Berber. The tribes that took part in the charge were the Duguaim, the Kenana, and Hamr Arabs from Kordofan; the Ja'alin and Metammeh men were kept in reserve. Most of them

Stewart's casualties at Abu Klea

	Officers		Other Ranks	
	K	W	K	W
Heavy Cavalry Camel Regiment	6	–	48	28
Light Cavalry Camel Regiment	1	3	8	9
Mounted Infantry	–	1	3	35
19th Hussars	–	–	2	4
35th (Royal Sussex)	–	–	5	25
Royal Artillery	–	2	–	2
Naval Brigade	2	2	6	9

▶ *The Battle of Abu Klea, 17 January 1885. Another version of the death of Colonel Fred Burnaby of The Blues, outside the square at Abu Klea.*

▶ *After the Battle of Abu Klea, Stewart's Desert Column, desperate for water, headed for the Nile. On 19 January 1885 they bivouacked at Abu Kru where they fought a successful action. Here the Camel Regiments are seen in their zareba.*

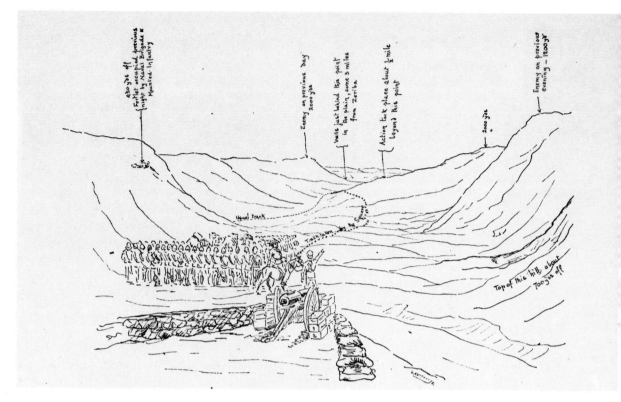

wore a white cotton robe wrapped around the waist with one end tied over the left shoulder; heads were shaved and a white cotton skull-cap was worn; the riflemen (mostly from the Mahdi's camp at Omdurman) wore the *jibbah*.

The Action at Abu Kru

At Abu Klea the 19th Hussars, who had been skirmishing to the right and left of the square, keeping a large body of enemy cavalry from working round behind it, were sent to the wells situated about four miles from the battle area. Using the Mounted Infantry as skirmishers, later in the day the re-formed square advanced and occupied the

wells, a series of holes in the sand on the valley floor. In turn the units filled bottles and water-skins and ensured that their camels had an adequate supply; great discipline and self-control was evident throughout. A cold and apprehensive night was spent in a hastily constructed zareba. Next morning, 18 January 1885, the force moved off, 19th Hussars leading, followed by Guards Camel Regiment, then baggage and ammunition, followed by the Heavy Camel Regiment and Mounted Infantry. They pressed on, marching through the night with occasional halts, the weary men losing formation and straggling so that the column stretched over two miles of desert. Early on 19 January the scouting cavalry discovered a native force $1^1/_2$ miles ahead, and further reconnaissance found an army pouring out of Metammeh. Hastily Stewart formed a zareba near Abu Kru, some four miles from the river; approaching, the enemy kept up a steady if erratic fire, causing many casualties including Stewart himself who was mortally wounded. Sir Charles Wilson, assuming command, took the desperate

◀ *The square forming-up outside their overnight zareba at Abu Kru before moving off in that formation to fight their way to the Nile.*

▼ *The Battle of Abu Kru. During the action General Sir Herbert Stewart was mortally wounded and had to be carried in a litter. He died on 16 February.*

course of marching his force out in square, intending to reach the Nile and entrench on the bank; he left 300 men with the guns and baggage in the zareba.

Supported at first by artillery fire from the zareba, the harassed force made slow progress and in two hours had covered only 1½ miles. Then two attacks came in on the left face and front of the formation. As courageously as at Abu Klea two days before, the Dervishes swept down on the square, in the teeth of a devastating fire that prevented any from coming nearer than 30 yards. After several attacks had been halted, the enemy gave up and withdrew.

In the advance from Abu Klea, the force had lost two officers and 22 men killed, nine officers and 92 men wounded. Desperately thirsty, the force did not reach the river at Gubat until nightfall, when the men fell like logs and buried faces in the muddy water. Gubat was occupied and its buildings loopholed for defence of the wounded and the supplies.

Wilson's Abortive Attack on Metammeh

On 21 January Wilson took 1,000 men and marched towards the town of Metammeh, four miles away, only to find it occupied by a large enemy force strongly entrenched. The beginnings of an attack were launched, but, realizing the town's strength, Wilson deemed it prudent to withdraw; the force returned to Gubat.

The Fall of Khartoum

During the next eight months scarcity gave way remorselessly to starvation, and hope to despair as from May to July the Mahdi's hordes closed in and tightened their grip on the city. In August one of Gordon's most capable soldiers, Muhammad Ali Pasha Husayn, led a number of successful sorties

► *Taking command of the Desert Force after General Stewart had been wounded, Sir Charles Wilson led 1,000 men to take the town of Metammeh on 21 January. Finding it strongly defended by entrenched Arabs, an attack was mounted but then called off and the force withdrew to Gubat.*

from the city, but early in September he was lured out of Khartoum and at al Aylafuh, twenty miles away, his force was overwhelmed and lost 1,000 Remington rifles. Gordon decided to try to take advantage of the prevailing high water of the Nile to send out the steamer *Abbas* carrying Colonel Stewart and Frank Power, correspondent of *The Times*, in an attempt to impress upon the world

outside the gravity of the situation. They never reached their destination; *Abbas* was captured between Abu Hamed and Merowe and they were taken by Arabs and treacherously murdered. At the end of September Gordon cut his links with the outside world by sending all his larger steamers to Shendi, to meet the expedition which he now knew was on its way. On 14 December Gordon sent his last message from the beleaguered city, saying that he could hold out for only ten more days; in fact it lasted for another six weeks.

As the level of the Nile receded the situation worsened; on 5 January 1885 Fort Omdurman on the far bank of the river capitulated, having been isolated for two months. This enabled the Mahdists to mount guns on the left bank of the White Nile to

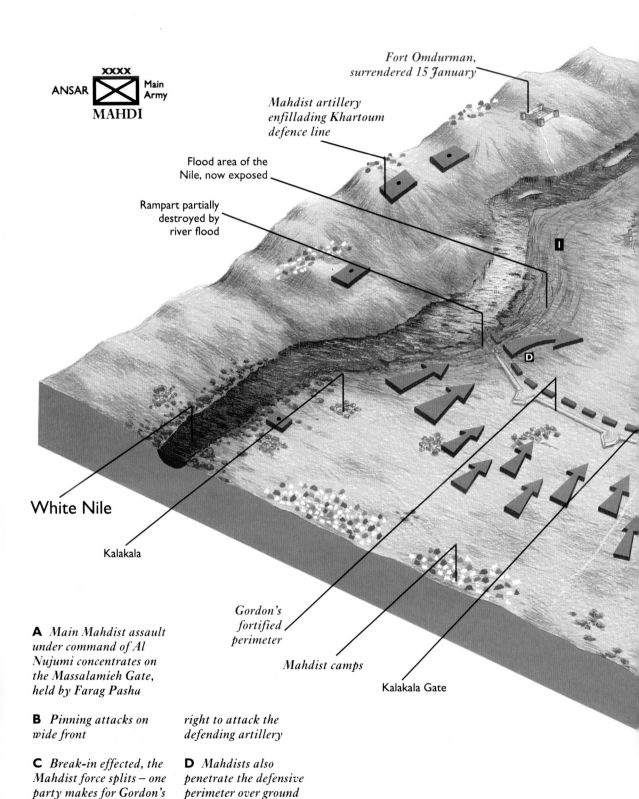

ANSAR **MAHDI** — xxxx — Main Army

Fort Omdurman, surrendered 15 January

Mahdist artillery enfillading Khartoum defence line

Flood area of the Nile, now exposed

Rampart partially destroyed by river flood

White Nile

Kalakala

Gordon's fortified perimeter

Mahdist camps

Kalakala Gate

A *Main Mahdist assault under command of Al Nujumi concentrates on the Massalamieh Gate, held by Farag Pasha*

B *Pinning attacks on wide front*

C *Break-in effected, the Mahdist force splits – one party makes for Gordon's headquarters, the other, and larger, force turns*

right to attack the defending artillery

D *Mahdists also penetrate the defensive perimeter over ground left dry by the fall of the Nile*

THE FALL OF KHARTOUM
26 January 1889, as seen from the south-east

EG ⊠ Garrison
GORDON

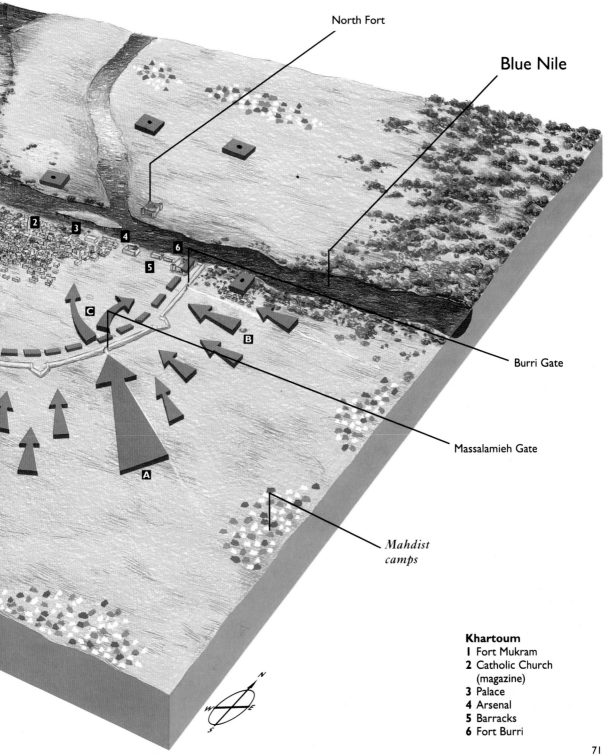

North Fort

Blue Nile

2

3

4

6

5

C

B

A

Burri Gate

Massalamieh Gate

*Mahdist
camps*

N
W — E
S

Khartoum
1 Fort Mukram
2 Catholic Church
(magazine)
3 Palace
4 Arsenal
5 Barracks
6 Fort Burri

◄ A fanciful representation of the death of Gordon, although there is no doubt that he faced his murderers in the resolute manner portrayed here.

enfilade the western end of Gordon's fortifications. As the river fell, muddy land began to appear beyond the end of the fortifications on the eastern shore until only a stretch of shallow water, lacking trenches, mines or wire entanglements, lay before the besiegers on the right flank of the defences. Soon after midnight on 26 January the assault began under cover of a general bombardment, and the attackers poured along the fortified line, bearing down all resistance and then rushing into the town to loot and massacre. A small party entered the Palace, Gordon's headquarters, where he is said to have met them at the top of the stairs; he was immediately cut down, and his head was removed and taken to the Mahdi. One of the most remarkable men of the Victorian era, Charles Gordon undoubtedly inspired his motley force with much of his own courage; of the same stuff as the early Christian martyrs, as a Christian martyr he died.

The River Steamers' Dash for Khartoum

At about the same time as Wilson called off the attack on Metammeh, the four river steamers sent

▲ *Sir Charles Wilson attempted to get Gordon out of Khartoum in a dash by the river steamers* Bordein *and* Telaha-wiya, *seen loading in this sketch by Melton Prior. The two boats carried 240 Egyptian and Sudanese soldiers plus 20 men of the Royal Sussex Regiment (in red tunics to impress the besiegers), seen here embarking.*

▶ *In the teeth of increasing hostile fire from the river banks, the steamers make their laborious way up the River Nile.*

down by Gordon from Khartoum were seen coming down the Nile. They bore messages indicating the critical situation in the besieged city, causing Wilson to decide to use two of them to make a dash for Khartoum and rescue Gordon. It took nearly three days to overhaul them, add protective armour and arrange crews — Lord Charles Beresford was in hospital and his Naval Brigade was depleted, so that crews had to be made up from the Sudanese of all

four vessels. On the morning of 24 January, carrying 240 Egyptian and Sudanese soldiers plus twenty men of the Royal Sussex Regiment, with red tunics to impress the besiegers, the *Bordein*, with Sir Charles Wilson aboard, and the *Telahwiya*, towing a barge laden with grain, set out from Gubat.

For three days, moving only in daylight, the little vessels made their way up the river which was exceptionally low at this time of year, frequently

◀ *In one of the steamers, a field gun in an improvised turret replies to enemy fire.*

▼ **Bordein** *rounds the bend at Tutti Island to find the city has fallen and Gordon is dead.*

▶ *Returning down the Nile, on 29 January* **Telahawiya** *strikes a rock and sinks. Her crew transfer to* **Bordein** *which in turn grounds at Mirnat Island and cannot be refloated. Wilson and his men scramble ashore and fortify the island, and a boat is sent to get help from Lord Charles Beresford at Metammeh.*

running aground, and engaging in fire-fights with natives on the banks; now and then it was necessary to stop, go ashore and pull down wooden houses to be used as fuel. On 28 January the city could be seen above the trees on Tutti Island; beyond that at the junction of the Blue and White Niles, they came under heavy fire and hundreds of natives could be seen lining the banks — obviously the city had fallen. Reluctantly Wilson gave the order to go

about and the ships ran at full speed down the Nile in what seemed to be an almost impossible bid to escape; but, with many casualties after hours of fighting, they passed beyond range of the Mahdists' guns.

On 29 January, approaching the sixth cataract, *Telahawiya* struck a rock and sank at Jebel Rowiyan, all on board transferring safely to *Bordein*; on 31 January *Bordein* grounded at Mirnat Island, some

forty miles above Gubat, and could not be refloated. Wilson and his party took refuge on the island while a small boat was rowed to Gubat for help, reaching there on 1 February; within a few hours Lord Charles Beresford set off in the small river steamer *Safieh* with a crew including twenty picked marksmen from the Rifles, two Gardners and two 4pdrs. On the third morning *Safieh* ran the gauntlet of Arab earthworks at Wadi Habashi, passing within 80 yards and pouring such a hail of bullets and shells into them that the defenders did not reply until the little steamer was 200 yards past them; then a lucky shell from an Arab gun went through the stern and into one of the boilers. Beresford managed to get the vessel further up-stream and anchored stern-on to the enemy at about 500 yards' range; throughout the day, as repair parties laboured furiously, a fire-fight ensued between boat and

◀ *Lord Charles Beresford in the river steamer* **Safieh** *on his way up-river to rescue Sir Charles Wilson from Mirnat Island.*

► Safieh *comes under heavy fire and is stopped in the water by a shell in one of her boilers. Anchoring stern-on to the enemy at a range of 500 yards, Beresford fights back for ten hours until the boiler has been repaired and the passage can be resumed.*

shore. Next morning at daybreak, the boiler having been repaired, Beresford was able to embark Wilson and his party who had descended the right bank. Without further mishap *Safieh* reached the camp of the Desert Column on the evening of 6 February.

On the same day, the Desert Column marched off into the desert, bearing their wounded, including General Stewart (who died on 16 February), arriving back at Korti in early March. Now the Mahdi reigned supreme from the Bayuda Desert to the far south, from the Red Sea hills to Darfur.

The Nile Column

While the Desert Column was marching and fighting its way to Gubat, the Nile or River Column under Major-General W. Earle was moving up-stream from Korti towards Abu Hamed, having left on 28 December 1884, the infantry in about 200 whale-boats and the mounted troops moving along the banks.

It took the Column four days to cover only seven miles of cataracts. Moving slowly, it passed through Merowe, then halted at Hamdah from 3 to 24 January. After ascending the fourth cataract, it reached Berti where, on 4 February, Earle heard of

the fall of Khartoum and was ordered to halt. On 8 February he was allowed to resume his advance.

The Battle of Kirbekan

Temporarily abandoning his boats, Earle began to march his force across the desert towards Abu Hamed, but on 10 February found his path blocked by about 2,000 warriors of the Ansar, positioned on

Earle's Nile (River) Column	
	Men
1st Bn, 38th (South Staffordshire Regiment)	600
2nd Bn, 56th (Essex Regiment)	740
1st Bn, 48th (Duke of Cambridge's Light Infantry)	650
1st Bn, 42nd (The Black Watch)	675
1st Bn, 75th (Gordon Highlanders)	750
1st Bn, 50th (Royal West Kent Regiment)	750
1st Bn, 78th (Royal Irish Regiment)	750
1st Bn, 79th (Cameron Highlanders)	500
8th (RR), 11th and 26th Coys, Royal Engineers	400
Naval Brigade	70
19th Hussars	350
Egyptian Camel Company	161
Egyptian Camel Battery (six 7pdrs)	120
Canadian Voyageurs and West African Kroomen	370
Egyptian soldiers (to haul the boats)	370

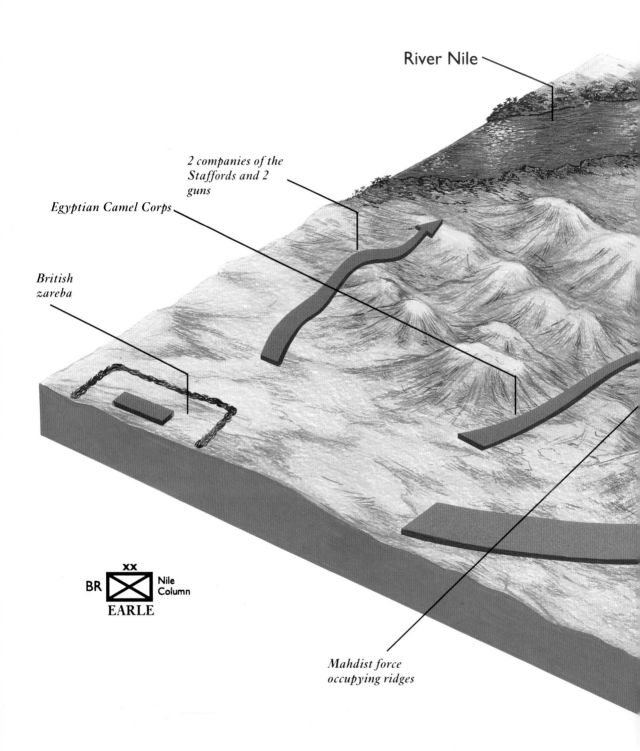

River Nile

2 companies of the
Staffords and 2
guns

Egyptian Camel Corps

British
zareba

BR | **xx** | Nile
EARLE | ⊠ | Column

Mahdist force
occupying ridges

THE BATTLE OF KIRBEKAN

10 February 1885, as seen from the south-west

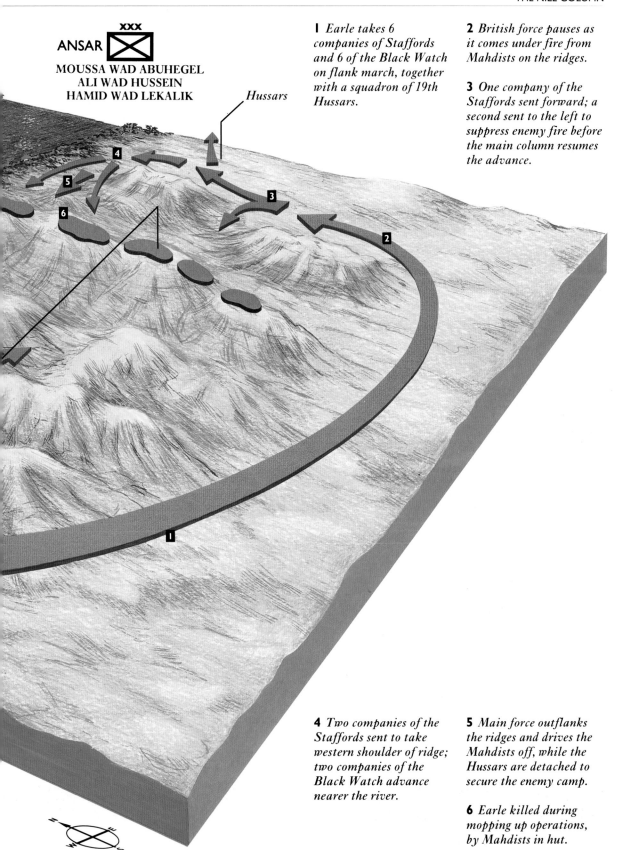

ANSAR XXX

MOUSSA WAD ABUHEGEL
ALI WAD HUSSEIN
HAMID WAD LEKALIK

Hussars

1 *Earle takes 6 companies of Staffords and 6 of the Black Watch on flank march, together with a squadron of 19th Hussars.*

2 *British force pauses as it comes under fire from Mahdists on the ridges.*

3 *One company of the Staffords sent forward; a second sent to the left to suppress enemy fire before the main column resumes the advance.*

4 *Two companies of the Staffords sent to take western shoulder of ridge; two companies of the Black Watch advance nearer the river.*

5 *Main force outflanks the ridges and drives the Mahdists off, while the Hussars are detached to secure the enemy camp.*

6 *Earle killed during mopping up operations, by Mahdists in hut.*

a ridge at Kirbekan. They were a mixed force, and included men of the Monassir tribe, some Robatat, and a group of Dervishes from Berber, commanded by Moussa wad Abuhegel, Ali wad Hussein and Hamid wad Lekalik all of whom were killed in the subsequent battle.

Earle planned to make a feigned frontal attack, while sending six companies each of the South Staffords and the Black Watch, together with the Hussars, around the enemy's left flank to take them in rear. Earle himself accompanied this party which, although seen and under fire for much of the way, got into position so as effectively to turn the enemy position and overlap it on the right flank. While searching the crest for Arabs hidden in holes or in clumps of rocks, they came upon a stone hut from which a rifleman shot and killed General Earle. Meanwhile, as the action progressed the guns of the false frontal attack could be heard by the infantry storming the heights to the skirl of the Highlanders' pipes.

Not needed in this attack, the Hussars rode off to capture the enemy's camp at the entrance to the nearby Shukool Pass. The operation at Kirbekan cost three officers and nine men killed, four officers and 43 men wounded; among the killed were General Earle, the commander of the column, and

Earle's force at Kirbekan

	Men
South Staffordshire Regiment	556
The Black Watch	437
19th Hussars (one squadron)	83
Egyptian Camel Company (½ company)	47
Egyptian Camel Battery (two guns)	24

Earle's casualties at Kirbekan

	Officers		Men	
	K	W	K	W
General Staff	1	–	–	–
38th (South Staffords)	1	2	5	22
42nd (Black Watch)	1	2	4	21

the commanding officers of both the infantry regiments engaged. Regimental breakdown was as shown above; enemy losses were said to number hundreds.

The End of the River Column

Command of the Column was taken over by General H. Brackenbury, CB, who continued the advance next day; on 17 February they reached Es Salamat, and on 20 February El Hebba, close to

where Colonel Stewart and Mr Powers from Khartoum had been murdered; the wreck of their steamer *Abbas* lay on a rock, and relics of the victims were found in a house. The mounted troops crossed the river and the Column moved on until, in the evening of 23 February, they had reached a point only 26 miles from Abu Hamed which they would probably have captured together with Berber had not General Wolseley ordered them back to Merowe on the following day. Arriving at Merowe on 5 March, the Column moved down-stream to reach Korti on 8 March and join hands with the travel-stained Desert Column; taking only nine days as against the 35 days it had taken to ascend the cataracts, although several lives were lost on the down-stream journey.

Before it was known that Khartoum had fallen, it was planned that Buller, now in command of the Desert Column, should move down the Nile and meet the River Column, while reinforcements from England landed at Suakim and marched to join them. But the Desert Column had achieved a masterly retirement from its position on the Nile near Metammeh, moving in square and repeatedly fending-off small-scale Arab attacks; they reached Korti on 16 March 1885.

Gordon was dead, Khartoum had fallen and the heart had gone out of the Nile Expedition. At Korti on 22 March, tents were struck and everyone set out for Cairo except a token force left at Tani, a few miles north of Ambukol on the Nile; this force eventually reached Cairo in mid-July.

◀ *On 10 February 1885 the River Column fought a battle at Kirbekan during which General Earle was killed by a shot fired from a stone hut (left of drawing; the spot where he was killed is marked with a + in the centre of the drawing).*

▶ *After the fall of Khartoum and the subsequent death of General Stewart of the Desert Column, General Sir Redvers Buller succeeded Sir Charles Wilson as commander. Buller extricated the Desert Column from their position on the Nile near Metammeh in a masterful withdrawal, marching in square and fending-off repeated Arab attacks, to arrive at Korti on 16 March 1885.*

FINAL OPERATIONS AROUND SUAKIM, FEBRUARY - MAY 1885

▲ *A Rating of the British Naval Brigade in the Sudan, 1884–5. His bayonet is the cutlass pattern for the Martini-Henry rifle. (Painting by Michael Roffe)*

After the withdrawal of the Desert and River Columns there was a renewed spasm of military activity which saw the arrival in Suakim on 12 March 1885 of a new expeditionary force under General Sir Gerald Graham, sent by Wolseley to protect the construction of a projected military railway from Suakim to Berber. It was a better-planned campaign than the first, with twice as many troops, battalions up to full strength, a balloon section, and colonial contingents from India and Australia. Totalling nearly 13,000 men, its composition was:

The port of Suakim was crowded with naval vessels, troopships, transports and hospital-ships, with special vessels for condensing 85,000 gallons of water daily. From Aden, Egypt and India were gathered 6,000 baggage and 500 riding-camels, with their headsmen and drivers; and mules from Cyprus, Gibraltar and Malta. It was said that fighting-men were almost lost in the multitude of camp-followers and the myriad of labourers working on the railway.

The Battle of Hashin

Graham's first task was to seek out and destroy Osman Digna's force of about 10,000 in the area Hashin-Tamai. He marched out on 20 March 1885 and, reaching a deserted village where Arabs fleetingly revealed themselves as the reconnaissance was carried out, the force encamped for the night. Next morning at 5 o'clock the troops were deployed in an open square with the Guards forming the right, marching in quarter columns of companies; 2 Brigade formed the front in columns of fours; native infantry on the left flank, with artillery, ambulance and transport in the centre; cavalry and mounted infantry were out in advance of the square. The Shropshires remained behind as a camp guard.

On 21 March, a very hot day, marching over

▲ *Despite Gordon's death and the fall of Khartoum, the British Government continued the campaign in the Sudan, a new expeditionary force being formed and sent to Suakim where it arrived on 12 March 1885, to fight under Graham. Among the reinforcements was a Guards Brigade under Major-General Lyon Fremantle, which was inspected at Windsor Castle by Queen Victoria before leaving for Egypt.*

Graham's force at Suakim, March 1885

	Men		Men
Guards Brigade		**Cavalry Brigade**	
(Major-General Lyon Fremantle)		(Major-General Sir Henry Ewart, KCB)	
1st Bn, Coldstream Guards	840	5th Royal Irish Lancers (two squadrons)	248
2nd Bn, Scots Guards	840	20th Hussars (two squadrons)	261
3rd Bn, Coldstream Guards	834	9th Bengal Cavalry (Hodson's Horse)	581
New South Wales Regiment	500	Mounted Infantry (four companies)	196
		Mounted Infantry Police	13
2 Infantry Brigade		**Artillery**	
(Major-General Sir John McNeill, VC, KCB)		6/B Royal Horse Artillery (six 9pdrs)	
1st Bn, 49th (Berkshires)	650	5/1 Scottish Divisional RA (mountain battery, six 2.5in guns)	
1st Bn, 53rd (Shropshires)	800	6/1 Ammunition Column, Scottish Divisional RA (equipped	
2nd Bn 70th (East Surreys)	600	with mules and camels; later manned Gardner guns on	
Royal Marine Light Infantry	500	armoured train)	
		Royal Engineers	
Indian Brigade		11th Coy, attached to Mounted Infantry	
(Brigadier-General J. Hudson, CB)		17th Coy	105
15th Ludhiana Sikhs	725	24th Coy	124
17th Bengal Native Infantry	843	10th Railway Company	
28th Bombay Native Infantry	245	2nd and 3rd Sections, Telegraph Battalion	
'F' Coy, Madras Sappers and Miners	150	Balloon Detachment	

◄ *The Battle of Hashin, 21 March 1885. Graham's new expeditionary force marched out of Suakim on 20 March, and on the following day came upon the enemy in a strong hilly position. In an action that dragged on for 9½ hours the British cavalry and mounted infantry made successful charges.*

The Battle of Hashin, 21 March 1885

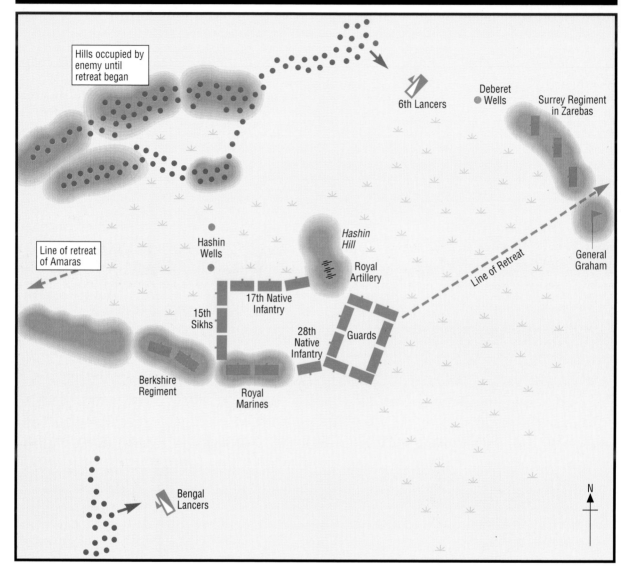

rough ground littered with boulders and prickly mimosa-grass, the force moved and fought for 9½ hours, both cavalry and infantry being repeatedly engaged. The Berkshires and Royal Marines drove the enemy off Dihilbat Hill, swarming up its steep sides in mutual support. The Indian Lancers charged a Dervish force and, as did the British cavalry at El Teb, they received a very rough handling from the natives, prone on the ground slashing at the horses' legs. The Indian infantry, in square with the Guards, inflicted heavy losses when repelling a fierce attack, which deterred another large group from charging. An attack by the cavalry

and Mounted Infantry was more successful, the troopers firing carbines at the natives lying on the dusty ground. Still the enemy fought on, banners waving and weapons flashing, occasional puffs of smoke betraying riflemen concealed in the mimosa bushes — the enemy were Beja, organized according to their tribal sections (Hadendowa, Bisharin, etc.) and fighting under their own leaders; estimates of their losses vary from 250 to 1,000 killed. When Graham's force got back to their prepared zarebas after the action, they counted their losses as 22 officers and men killed, and 43 wounded.

McNeill's Zareba at Tofrik, 22 March 1885

Next day, General Graham sent out a strong force under General McNeill to build and garrison two zarebas as intermediate supply posts between Hashin and Tamai. Formed in two supporting squares, they advanced slowly through dense scrub and mimosa-bush, but by midday had only reached Tofrik, six miles from Suakim, where he decided to build the first post; the second one was to be eight miles further on. Three zarebas of mimosa-thorn were begun, placed diagonally in chequer-board fashion, the larger central one to house the animals and stores, the two smaller ones to hold the fighting troops and the Gardner guns. The 5th Lancers were

out forming a protective screen and scouting party; unfortunately they were a young regiment with no experience of desert warfare and unused to the glaring sun light of the region.

The northern flanking square was being constructed by Royal Marines, with two Gardner guns; the Berkshires, also with two Gardners, were working on the southern square — both had arms piled. At 2 o'clock, when the men fell out for the midday meal, there was no adequate field of fire around the incomplete defences. The Indian units were in the area of the unfinished central square, where camels and mules were assembled after off-loading.

At 2.30 p.m. a cavalryman galloped in and

The Battle of Tofrik, 22 March 1885

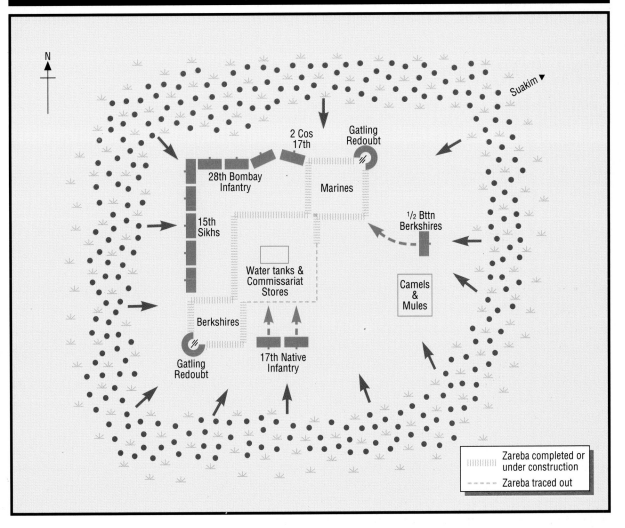

reported that enemy were approaching rapidly; covering and working-parties were ordered in, but before they could comply the cavalry outposts were among them with Sudanese swarming at their heels; thousands of gleaming black Hadendowas who seemed to have sprung, screaming and shouting, from the very ground. Engulfed by this flood of hacking, stabbing natives, men dashed for their rifles; the 17th Bengal Native Infantry fired a volley then broke and rushed for shelter in the central zareba. General McNeill was lucky to escape with his life when the main attack hit the Berkshires' zareba, but a group of men from that regiment formed a rallying-square outside the middle zareba, and held their fire until the Arabs were within thirty yards. They mowed down the tribesmen milling around their small formation before slowly falling back on the Marines' zareba, frequently halting to fire volleys at from two to twenty yards' range.

In the first rush some sixty Arabs penetrated the Marines' square, to be instantly shot or bayoneted; but an avalanche of warriors, fleeing Indian infantry, camp-followers and terrified animals burst through the central square, carrying away many of those men who had formed defensive positions. With the natives now among the transport animals, the Berkshires and Marines had to fire their heavy volleys into the mass, and camels reared their great bodies into the air before slumping, shapeless tawny hummocks, on the blood-soaked sand. The whole area became a dust-enshrouded nightmare of shouting demoralized men, frantic camels and plunging mules, and the wraith-like Hadendowas flitting through the murk, cleaving paths with their long, razor-sharp swords.

Remaining firm, the 15th Sikhs and 28th Bombay Infantry received and repulsed several attacks; thrown back, the Arabs milled about in all directions, slashing at anything that moved. At last, unable to cope with the concentrated fire of the Berkshires and Marines in their zarebas, the surviving Arabs slowly and sullenly moved off and walked slowly away into the bush.

Lasting only twenty minutes, the chaotic action had been crowded with instances of wild and desperate fanaticism, tempered by examples of cold-blooded bravery. As the dust slowly settled men

Stewart's casualties at Tofrik				
	Officers		Men	
	K	W	K	W
Naval Brigade	1	1	6	5
5th Lancers	1	–	–	5
Royal Artillery	–	1	–	4
Royal Engineers	2	1	13	3
Berkshires	1	–	22	30
Royal Marines	–	–	71	6
Madras Sappers and Miners	2	1	12	20
15th Sikhs	–	–	9	11
17th Bombay Regiment	1	1	20	33

looked at one another in bewilderment before gazing around them at the shambles of bodies of men and animals lying on all sides. More than a hundred British and Indian soldiers had died and about 140 were wounded; 900 camels had been destroyed. Estimates of the Sudanese casualties vary depending on the source, but it seems that at least 1,000 bodies were lying in the area after the battle, and it is claimed that 2,000 were buried in grave-pits. As always, the enemy fought with extraordinary and fanatical courage, showing a complete disregard for death; but even by their standards the affair at Tofrik was so bloody that they were discouraged from further attacks, and were beginning to lose confidence in Osman Digna who had told them that British bullets were made of water and could do them no harm.

The End of the Campaign

For some days after the Tofrik action military operations were confined to marching and counter-marching, convoy escorts and skirmishes with bands of belligerent Arabs. On 2 April 1885 Graham marched with a strong force from Suakim to attack Osman Digna at Tamai, reaching there on the following day only to find the place deserted and the wells almost dry. Most of the tribes supporting Osman had left him, and the leader was on his way to Sinkat; it was clear that the campaign was nearly at an end.

On 2 May Lord Wolseley arrived at Suakim to warn Graham that his force was to be broken up because the government had decided to abandon Suakim and discontinue construction of the railway; besides, there was a possibility of trouble with

Russia. Graham left Suakim on 17 May by which time Korti had been abandoned and the withdrawal was in full swing; in June Wolseley and Graham were back in England

In June the Mahdi died, probably of typhus. Before his death Osman Digna had written to him: 'God struck fear into the hearts of the English and they went away.' The power of the Dervishes was supreme in the land and British prestige was at a low ebb. However the British Lion refused to lie down; one last action was fought, significant for the fact that it was the very last occasion on which British soldiers wore their scarlet tunics into battle. The Mahdi's successor, the Khalifa, had been raiding in the vicinity of British outposts at Kosha and Mograka, on the Egyptian/Sudanese border. On 30 December 1885, General Sir Frederick Stephenson, with two Anglo-Egyptian brigades supported by cavalry, and gunboats on the Nile, defeated the Khalifa's forces at Ginnis, with fewer than fifty casualties and only a few hundred to the enemy.

Britain had the habit of withdrawing only to return — as in Bengal, Burma and Afghanistan. She followed the custom in the Sudan, her troops returning to avenge Gordon and Khartoum in Kitchener's Campaign of 1896-8.

▼ McNeill's zareba at Tofrik, 22 March 1885. General Graham had sent out a strong force under General McNeill to build and garrison two zarebas between Hashin and Tamai. Before they were completed the force was *surprised by a large army of Dervishes who had crept up under cover of dense scrub. For twenty minutes a ferocious battle was fought amid the incomplete zarebas and transport animals.*

CHRONOLOGY

1881 Appearance of the Mahdi
August Mahdi's victory at Abba
October Mahdi defeats Rashid Bey
1882
29 May Mahdists defeat Egyptians at Jebel Jarrada
1 September Mahdists besiege El Obeid
1883
1 January Colonel Hicks appointed Chief of Staff of Egyptian Army
17 El Obeid falls
29 April Hicks's victorious action at Jebel Ain
9 September Hicks marches out of Omdurman to recapture El Obeid
26 October Mahdists destroy an Egyptian force
5 November Hicks's army destroyed at Shaykan; Mahdists destroy another Egyptian force
2 December Mahdists wipe out an Egyptian force; Slatin Pasha cut off in Darfur; Baker Pasha's force assembles at Suakim

1884
January Lupton defeated at Bahr-el-Gazal in Equatoria; Emin Pasha retreats up the Nile
10 Baring, in Cairo, rejects Gordon as Governor of Sudan
15 Wolseley interviews Gordon at War Office
18 Gordon meets Cabinet. Later that day leaves London for Cairo
25 In Cairo, Gordon meets Baring and Tewfik
26-7 Baker Pasha's force transported by sea to Trinkatat
28 Gordon leaves Cairo for Khartoum with Lieutenant-Colonel J.D.H. Stewart
1 February They reach Korosko
4 Baker's force routed near Trinkatat
8 Admiral Hewitt lands British force at Suakim, with orders to mount expedition to relieve Tokar
10 Gordon sends Mahdi red robe of honour
13 British troops in Egypt begin embarking for Suakim
18 Gordon and Stewart reach Khartoum
23 Tokar surrenders
28 Graham's force from Suakim concentrates at Trinkatat
29 Graham wins Battle of El Teb; Colonel Stewart and Mr Power make two-steamer reconnaissance of White Nile from Khartoum
2 March Stewart and Power return to Khartoum
3 Graham's force reaches Tokar
5 Graham's force returns to Suakim
12 Graham's force marches out to Tamai
13 Graham victorious at Battle of Tamai; telegraph from Khartoum to Cairo cut by Mahdists; tribes north of Khartoum rise in support of Mahdi, Khartoum cut off
14 Rebels occupy positions on right bank of Blue Nile opposite palace at Khartoum
15 Besieged garrison of Hafayah north of Khartoum relieved by Gordon's river force
16 Abortive sortie from Khartoum — 200 killed; British government refuses Gordon's request that Zobeir be appointed Governor-General of Sudan
20 Khartoum besieged by Arab army of 30,000
22 Mahdi rejects Gordon's offer of peace
24 Baring in Cairo telegraphs London on importance of getting Gordon out of Khartoum
28 Graham's force at Suakim ordered to return to Egypt, leaving garrison of two battalions
3 April Graham's force embarks for Egypt
9 Graham's force reaches Cairo
9 May Berber falls
10 Messengers confirm Khartoum under tight siege and out of contact
12 Government survives vote of censure over their attitude and inactivity concerning Gordon and Khartoum
17 Government message reaches Gordon advising evacuation of Khartoum
20 Public indignation in England at 'betrayal of

Gordon' increases and continues throughout June and July
10 Confirmation of fall of Berber and massacre of the garrison
26 July Lord Hartingdon tells Gladstone he will resign unless help is sent to Gordon
5 August Government votes funds for a relief expedition
8 Gladstone gives way, announces plan for expedition to the Sudan, commander Lord Wolseley; general diversion of British regiments en route to and from India to Wadi Halfa; Muhammad Ali Pasha Husayn leads successful sorties from Khartoum
24 Letters from Gordon received, reporting minor actions with Arabs from 12 March to 30 July; Gordon says he has received no letters since 29 March
26 Another letter from Gordon announces a victory, having taken an Arab camp Khartoum is 'cleared on three parts of a circle'; General Sir Redvers Buller leaves England for Egypt
28 Eight hundred whale-boats ordered for Nile expedition
4 September Expedition sent from Khartoum to Sennar defeated with loss of 800 men at Al Aylafuh
9 Wolseley arrives in Cairo
10 First boats ready and delivered in England; steamer *Abbas* strikes rock, Stewart and Power go ashore and are murdered by apparently friendly Arabs
20 Gordon receives first news that relief expedition is on its way
27 Wolseley leaves Cairo for Wadi Halfa
7 October Canadian Voyageurs arrive in Alexandria
14 Gordon arrests sixteen leading citizens who have planned to go over to the Mahdi
21 Mahdi moves to Khartoum with bulk of his forces
22 Gordon receives letter from Mahdi telling of wreck of *Abbas* and death of Stewart and Powers
5 December Relief force assembles at Donga
15 Steamer *Bordein* under heavy fire leaves Khartoum for Metammeh; Gordon sends last message; General Stewart arrives at Korti with Mounted Infantry and Guards Camel Corps
16 Wolseley arrives at Korti
28 River Column leaves Korti and advances towards Khartoum
30 Stewart's Desert Column leaves Korti to take wells at Gakdul

1885
1 January First boats bearing The Black Watch reach Korti
2 Desert Column occupies wells at Gakdul
3 General Earle joins advance-guard of River Column
4 South Staffords pass cataract and occupy Hamdah; joined by River Column who camp there before moving forward; General Earle arrives Hamdah with his Staff
5 Lord Charles Beresford reaches Korti with 1st Division, Naval Brigade; Desert Column returns to Korti; in Khartoum commander of Fort Omdurman signals Gordon that he can longer hold out, Gordon agrees to his surrender
7 Colonel Clarke with Light Camel Regiment leaves Korti for Gakdul
8 Stewart's Desert Column marches out of Korti
13 United, the entire Column moves forward
16 Large Arab force discovered at Abu Klea wells
17 Stewart's force defeats Arabs at Abu Klea
18 Column begins march to Metammeh
19 General Stewart mortally wounded, Sir Charles Wilson takes command; Column sights Nile. Here at Abu Kru (Gubat), Stewart wounded
20 Force concentrates at Gubat
21 Wilson makes abortive attack on Metammeh; contact made with four river steamers sent down by Gordon
24 River Column leaves Hamdah; Wilson takes party from Desert Column up Nile in steamers *Bordein* and *Talahawiyeh*
25-6 Mahdi's forces attack Khartoum, city falls and Gordon is killed; Wilson's force in *Bordein* go aground en route to Khartoum
26 *Bordein* refloated
27 Buller, with Royal Irish Regiment, begins march to Gubat
28 Wilson's steamers arrive at junction of Blue and White Niles; *Bordein* leads way into Khartoum, heavily engaged from shore; finding Khartoum in enemy hands, Wilson orders retreat
29 Steamer *Talahawiyeh* hits rocks and sinks
31 At cataract near Wadi Habashi *Bordein* hits rocks

and is abandoned; force camps on nearby island; small boat rows forty miles for assistance

1 February Boat reaches Gubat. Lord Charles Beresford sets out in steamer *Safieh* to find Wilson

3 *Safieh* damaged by fire from shore; after repair carries on to reach Wilson

4 Beresford finds Wilson and returns to Korti with him and his party; Desert Column concentrates at Berti

5 Force ordered to halt on hearing of fall of Khartoum; London hears of fall of Khartoum and death of Gordon

6 Steamer *Safieh* reaches Desert Column camp

8 Earle ordered by Wolseley to push on to Abu Hamed. Earle decides to abandon boats and march across desert

9 On being told that a force is to be detailed for an advance to Suakim, Wolseley asks for an Indian Brigade and a cavalry force

10 Buller and Royal Irish Regiment arrive at Gubat from Korti; Nile Column wins Battle of Kirbekan; Earle is killed, General Brackenbury takes command

17 General Stewart dies of wounds received on 19 January; River Column's march resumed, they reach Es Salamat

19 Queen Victoria inspects Grenadier Guards at Windsor before their departure for the Sudan

20 Brackenbury's force reaches El Hebba

23 Buller evacuates Abu Klea

24 Brackenbury within 26 miles of Abu Hamed

26 Buller's column reaches Gakdul

4 March Brackenbury's forces arrive at Hamdah

5 They reach Merowe and Brackenbury holds final review of River Column

7 He leaves with main body for Korti

8 Desert Column sets out for Korti

12 General Graham arrives in Suakim

16 Construction of Suakim-Berber railway line begun; Desert Column reaches Korti

20 Graham's force begins advance from Suakim to Hashin

21 Graham victorious at Battle of Hashin

22 Graham's force surprised at Tofrik; wins hard-fought battle; troops leave Korti for Cairo

29 Australian Contingent arrives at Suakim

1 April Graham's force advances to Tamai — no enemy there

4 Graham's force returns to Suakim

2 May Wolseley arrives at Suakim

17 General Graham and his Staff embark from Suakim

19 Wolseley and Staff embark from Suakim; Australians embark for home

2 June Australian Contingent arrives Sydney

8 Wolseley and General Graham back in London

29 Death of Mahdi

6 July British forces reassemble in Egypt

A GUIDE TO FURTHER READING

ALEXANDER, Michael. *The True Blue.* (Life of Colonel Fred Burnaby). 1957

ARCHER, Thomas. *The War in Egypt and the Soudan. 1886-7*

BERESFORD, Admiral Sir Charles. *Memoirs.* 1914

Brackenbury, Major-General Henry. *The River Column.* 1885

BUTLER, Sir William. *Campaign of the Cataracts. 1887*

FEATHERSTONE, Donald. *Colonial Small Wars, 1837-1901.* 1973

— *Weapons and Equipment of the Victorian Soldier.* 1978

— *Victoria's Enemies - An A-Z of British Colonial Warfare.* 1989

GLEICHEN, Count. *With The Camel Corps up the Nile.* 1888

GRANT, James. *Cassell's History of the War in the Soudan.* 1887

HOLT, P.M. *The Mahdist State in the Sudan, 1881-1889.* 1971

JACKSON, E.C. *Osman Digna.* 1926

MANFIELD, Peter. *The British in Egypt.* 1971

MOOREHEAD, Alan. *The White Nile.* 1960

— *The Blue Nile.* 1962

PRESTON, Adrian (ed.). *In Relief of Gordon.* (Lord Wolseley's Campaign Journal of the Khartoum Relief Expedition, 1884-5). 1967

SANDES, E.W.C. *The Royal Engineers in Egypt and the Sudan.* 1937

SHAKED, H. *The Life of the Sudanese Mahdi.* 1978

SHIBEIKA, Mekki. *British Policy in the Sudan, 1882-1902.* 1952

STACEY, Colonel C.P. *Records of the Nile Voyageurs, 1884-5.* 1959

THEOBALD, A.B. *The Mahdiya.* 1951

WINGATE, F.R. *Mahdism and the Egyptian Sudan.* 1891

ZULFO, 'Ismat Hasan. (trans. Peter Clark). Karari. (Sudanese account of Omdurman with much on the Mahdi and Mahadiyya). 1980

Illustrated London News, 1881-6

WARGAMING THE SUDAN CAMPAIGNS

'The sand of the desert is sodden red,
  Red with the wreck of a square that broke;
  The Gatling's jammed and the Colonel dead,
  And the Regiment blind with dust and smoke.'

These lines from Sir Henry Newbolt's *Vitai Lampada* , written at the end of the 19th century, refer to that most evocative of all colonial wars — the Sudan Expedition to get Gordon out of Khartoum and the Battle of Abu Klea, fought on 17 January 1885. The Colonel was 'True Blue' Fred Burnaby of The Blues, in the desert on 'sick-leave', who liked fighting outside the square with a double-barrelled 12-bore shotgun loaded with pig-shot; and it was a Gardner gun that jammed, not a Gatling. Four lines that stir the imagination and tingle the spine as they suggest what it was like to be a British soldier in a small, inadequately equipped expedition, taking on vastly superior numbers of Dervishes, fanatical fighters in their own peculiarly alien terrain, with annihilation the only alternative to victory.

To any British wargamer worthy of his salt, it cries out to be reproduced on a wargames table, with scaled-down armies of model soldier accurately painted to represent the British soldier of the Victorian era, and colourful semi-naked opponents of the Hadendowa, Beja, Bisharin or a host of other tribes of that hot and barren African country. Providing scope for dashing, perhaps even outrageous rules, it is the territory of the outrageous wargamer, the 'chancer' or gambler, the player whose nature or temperament possibly make him out-of-place among more orthodox modes of warfare. Such a wargamer will be in his element as he controls large numbers of mobile native warriors, flitting hither and thither about the table.

Such a player will disdain the complaint of inequality that tends to discourage less dashing wargamer from handling native armies; he delights in skilfully employing every inch of movement bestowed upon them by the rules, always bearing in mind how the Mahdists wiped out the forces of Billy Hicks and Baker Pasha, and nursing as his touchstone the Zulu victory at Isandhlwana in 1879 — believing all these things to be well within his reach on the wargames table. Or he might fancy himself as the heroic leader of a far smaller force, effectively massing his extra firepower while demonstrating the coolness, courage and control of a Roberts or a Wolseley; maybe he will take on the mantle of General Charles Gordon in a simulated siege of Khartoum, employing ingenious ideas and devices resembling those of Baden-Powell at Mafeking that will bring despair to the rule-compilers — and his opponents.

The principal feature of wargaming colonial wars is the necessity of ensuring through the rules and careful balancing of numbers that the British force is in with a chance against perhaps six or seven times its own strength — and it must be done in a spirit of historical accuracy and authenticity. The superior military technology that ensured victory on the historical day must be reproduced in miniature by the weapons placed in the hands of our combatants, and the potentialities bestowed upon them by the rules in use. This mean that the compilers of those rules, and ideally those using them, have studied the period until they possess a deep working knowledge of it in all its military aspects.

Perhaps the best means of grafting upon smaller, disciplined forces the ability to withstand the onslaught of far greater numbers is to employ the *morale* factor —that nebulous quality which in real life determines whether a man or a regiment stands firm when others are breaking. Unlike humans, our little model armies do not possess this faculty; it has to be given them via the rules controlling the game, and in colonial warfare the higher morale of the soldier that has been drilled into him by discipline and boring routines is bestowed upon the regiments and the army to a higher tangible degree than it is to the tribesmen. For them, a morale-ruling that can fluctuate and allow them to display incredible and fanatical bravery tinged with the possibility that — suddenly — they might break and run. Allied to this is the ruling governing 'uncontrolled charges', simulating their innate impetuosity that might cause them to hurl themselves into a courageous but reckless attack at a tactically unsound moment. Also part of the 'morale' aspects of colonial warfare is the undoubted and oft-occurring occasion when the morale of a native group or force plummets at the death of a chieftain or leader

Acknowledging that the outstanding feature of colonial warfare and wargaming lies in the disparity in numbers, i.e., lack of numerical balance, this has to be simulated on the miniature battlefield in such a way as to ensure that both sides have a reasonable chance of winning, and that such near-Ansar successes as Tamai or Tofrik can be transformed into the victory they so nearly achieved. This is done by allowing the smaller, disciplined force advantageous rules to simulate their superior tactical formations and enhanced firepower; while the natural mobility of the natives is simulated by longer move-distances than the British, and their natural fanaticism and ferocity at close-quarters fighting is represented by giving them superior values in hand-to-hand fighting (mêlées), but only after they have surmounted the volume of fire they must take as they attempt to make contact with the formed ranks of the disciplined ranks of the soldiers. And do not forget to grant facilities to native foes that allow them the boon of surprise and ambush, perhaps by allowing their initial positions on the table to be indicated on sketch-maps of the terrain, rather than them being forced to set themselves out in full view of the enemy; the rules stating that they must reveal themselves when opposing forces come within an agreed distance — perhaps the natives' move-distance.

In most cases natives hated cavalry, particularly lancers, and many sets of rules for colonial wargaming make it difficult for them to stand firm when attacked by a mounted unit and, when they break and are pursued, they are given a much reduced defensive capability. As can be deduced from accounts of such battles as El Teb, Sudanese warriors more than held their own against cavalry, it being said that mounted men usually came off worse when charging into masses of them. So, when making rules to re-fight the battles described in this book, give the Dervish parity with the lancer.

The almost contemptuous bravery shown by native enemies in the Sudan could give the impression that they might take artillery fire in their stride. However, the belching guns and their explosive and deadly missiles must have been so alien to them as to be heartily disliked, as artillery was to all relatively unsophisticated foes. Rules should reflect this by making them break more easily when under artillery fire, to back-off out of range or seek cover. The same thing must apply to the chattering, if oft-jamming Gatling and Gardner guns, whose effect can equate with the musketry of an infantry battalion per gun; a touch of realism that brings amusement (and frustration) to a colonial wargame is to rule that each machine-gun should throw a dice and be made to jam if not reaching a stipulated score.

The most suitable scale of figure to use in Sudanese games is the 15mm range, because if military scaling is to be accurate, there has to be a very large number of natives on the table and, should the scaled figures be larger, they will be grouped together in an unreal manner, making a far better target than presented in real life. Wide-ranging varieties of figures of this campaign are available from a number of manufacturers, both in Britain and the USA, and the ubiquitous British infantryman, painted perhaps in a slightly different uniform, can be taken from ranges covering the Zulu War; Afghanistan; India and the Transvaal War of 1881.

It is not unfair to say that the period under discussion in this book is probably as good as any colonial era, with a colourful and courageous foe against whom the British had only a slight superiority in types of weapons, assuming that the enterprising wargamer allows his Ansar army to employ modern weapons captured from defeated Egyptian troops, manned by their normal trained crews, captured and impressed into service. Battles can be reasonably large, but might be slow-moving unless the British are given an objective, with a time-limit, to avoid them forming square and sitting tight awaiting attack; an ideal objective can be the need for the British to reach the Nile, or capture wells, so as to survive; lack of water would affect their performance.

Living as we do in an age when the use of such words as 'uncivilized', 'barbarians' or 'savages' causes ethnic groups to accuse authors of being 'racists', it is not beyond the bounds of possibility that accusing fingers might be pointed at tabletop representations of those numerous historical occasions when natives defending their homelands were massacred in large numbers as they learned the painful lesson that sheer courage can never prevail in the face of superior military technology. Perhaps there is some mitigation in the knowledge shared by most wargamers and military historians that, despite suffering at least 100 casualties to every ten sustained by their European enemy, these ill-armed natives invariably revealed incredible courage and dignity, defeated solely through being overtaken by the March of Civilized Progress. Wargames rules thoughtfully reflect their courage and, as there is no enjoyment in playing a game where the same side invariably wins, the best man always triumphs in these tabletop affairs — and it is the native more often than not.